KU-516-326

FIRST CONTACT

FIRST CONTACT

A 21ST CENTURY DISCOVERY OF CANNIBALS

Mark Anstice

Published by Eye Books

Copyright © Mark Anstice 2004

All rights reserved. Apart from brief extracts for the purpose of review, no part of this publication may be reproduced, stored in a retrieval system, or transmitted in any form or by any means, electronic, mechanical, photocopying, recording or otherwise without the permission of the publisher.

Mark Anstice has asserted his right under the Copyright, Designs and Patents Act 1988 to be identified as the author of this work.

First Contact
1st Edition
April 2004

Published by Eye Books Ltd
51a Boscombe Rd
London
W12 9HT
Tel/fax: +44 (0) 20 8743 3276
website: www.eye-books.com

Set in Frutiger and Garamond
ISBN: 1903070260

British Library Cataloguing in Publication Data
A catalogue record for this book is available from the British Library

Printed and bound in Great Britain by Biddles Ltd, King's Lynn

Front cover flap photographs:

Top: Bapa Tua 1, Lukun
Centre: Bruce and Mark after talking about each other to the camera
Bottom: Una girl, Lukun

To the people of Irian Jaya, and in memory of Wandy Swales,
the man whose expeditions introduced me to Indonesia.

Acknowledgements

I am indebted to Vanessa Aistrup, Jan Still, Alastair Tindal, Sonny Supriyadi, and Hazel Orme for their support, assistance and editing, and especially to my parents, Michael and Carolyn Anstice - without their support I would have struggled to write this book. Thank you also to Bruce Parry, for inviting me along in the first place.

Contents

Map of Irian Jaya

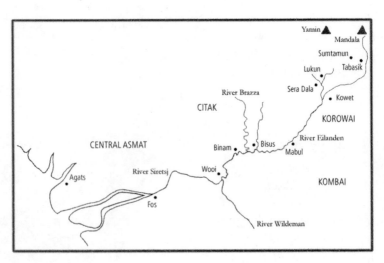

PREFACE: 24 JANUARY 2000

As I sit down now to write up the events and thoughts of the last week, it is with a heavy sense of resignation. I have lost my diary of our journey to date – forever it seems. It only amounted to some eighty pages and I can, I suppose, piece together from memory the trials and tribulations of the last five weeks. What really irks me, though, is that the first diary I have ever succeeded in writing diligently is not truly lost. I know exactly where I left it, where it is now, and who is now fingering the pages.

The young Korowai tribesman called Yakop, surely by now returned from his pig-hunting trip, will be in his hut sheltering from the rain and wondering whether or not those bizarre white men will return for the book. His own language has no word for 'book' but Yakop, unlike the other men from his tiny village, has had some dealings with the outside world and speaks a little 'Bahasa Indonesia'. He also understands the value of money so will probably also be wondering if it is worth as much to me as the price of a steel *parang* (machete) for him.

Alternatively, he has discovered that paper makes excellent tinder.

But Yakop's possible conversion to capitalism is not what keeps me from retracing our steps of the last few days – it's the rain. It fell all last night and is now once more hammering its way though the grass roof above my head like a ceaseless drum roll announcing the arrival of the wet season.

On the map, the two crosses that mark the locations of Yakop's hut and that of our host here are merely an inch apart – just one full day's walk through relatively easy jungle. Between them, however, meanders a cluster of tiny blue lines that fall magnificently short of describing adequately the Eilanden river at this point. Three quarters of a mile wide and split into nineteen different watercourses, it's a monster. Bruce and I have crossed it twice in the last ten days and on both occasions were swept away and almost drowned. That was where it was at its smallest and weakest. Now it is being fed on a vast scale and we have probably only just made it back to the rest of our food and equipment in time. I have tried all morning to recruit a local Una tribesman to help me make the journey again but all are adamant that it's no longer possible. The rainy season has arrived. That doesn't mean it wasn't raining before, just that it's going to rain every day now. They don't really have a dry season here, only varying degrees of wet.

But if truth be told, relief is mixed with my annoyance. In the six days since we left Pondok Jon there has been a solid possibility of getting my scribblings back. Yakop and his cronies, last seen squatting in the gloom beneath the *pondok's* rotting roof, clutching their bows and arrows, watching our departure through indifferent eyes, would have discovered the diary as soon as they stood up to leave, and our respective forays into that part of the forest would, Yakop knew, both return to Kowet.

On our way back we waited an extra day for him, staying in his hut. I couldn't ask Bruce to hang around any longer, not with our food just two days walk away, and God only knew how long a pig hunt might take. With a lot of sign language and quite a bit of grunting, I gathered from one of Kowet's inhabitants that if you are hunting to kill, it doesn't take so long, but if you want to capture the pigs alive for domestication then you can be gone for ages.

So we returned here to Sera Dala. If it were possible, I would go back, leaving Bruce to find some new porters for our onward journey. He knows this and has been understanding about the whole situation but I'm glad now not to be holding up the expedition any longer. Our visas and travel permits run out in a week, we have a mountain to climb, and small notion of how to get to it.

Finally, my right foot is in tatters. Ceaseless immersion in river and swamp has largely stripped it of skin while, startlingly, leaving the nerve endings in tip-top working condition. That the left remains perfectly healthy does nothing to make the prospect of heading back into the swamp any more appealing.

I have built a desk in the corner of this hut using two bags of dehydrated rations and a plank and must now make an aide-memoire of the events that have brought us this far. And there's so much new stuff to write about. I can hardly believe that we have made 'first contact' with a new clan of the Korowai. The more I think about it, the more I realise how lucky we were not to have been killed and eaten. Not that they would have found much meat on us. I have never worked so physically hard or eaten so little for so long. Thank God we are back with our food. Bruce keeps wandering in to my little 'office', trying to tempt me into raiding one of the bags again, but I am already full. We have been on a starvation ration of baked, unripe bananas for too long and that my desk is made partly of 'chicken and pasta' and partly of 'four seasons' casserole', albeit in powder form, is distraction enough. I can barely concentrate on what it was that made me want to hump a huge rucksack around Irian Jaya in the first place.

PART 1

1 RELIEF DATA INCOMPLETE

The call could not have come at a better time really. On Monday mornings my office seemed more confining than usual. It was eight feet long by five feet wide. Few people knew that; the voices and telephones of the businesses beyond the partition screens gave my clients, when they phoned, the impression that they were dealing with a larger company. In the mail there had been a large poster of the Namib desert sent by an African tour operator to inspire the staff they thought I had. The only place to hang it was already occupied by an optimistically large spreadsheet entitled 'Confirmed Bookings'. When the phone rang I was wondering vaguely which would most inspire me.

I picked up the receiver. 'Maverick Travel, good morning.'

It was Bruce Parry. 'The expedition, are you still up for it?' he said immediately, 'I think we have our sponsorship. They want us to come in and talk about it tomorrow morning at nine. Can you make it?'

'Absolutely.'

'Good. We'll go over everything tonight. We'll only get one shot at this.'

After the call I sat motionless for a long time, smiling. This was probably going to cripple me financially but I didn't care; I was on the brink of the greatest adventure of my life.

Bruce Parry had been the leader of an expedition in Sumatra that I had joined, in the capacity of project manager, shortly after I left the Army in 1995. He had served in the Royal Marine Commandos and had the distinction of having been the youngest officer ever to command the legendary Physical Training School at Lympstone. The expeditions he led for a youth development charity were chiefly science-oriented, involving static projects, but the job had taken him all over the Indonesian archipelago and he had developed a passion for the country and its people. As we walked in single file along narrow jungle paths we had compared ideas for future expeditions, selfish ones where adventure was the only goal. Bruce wanted to cross 'Irian Jaya', an almost mythical place where the jungle was rumoured to be some of the least hospitable on the planet, and clung to almost vertical slopes amid a never-ending labyrinth of dark valleys. Irian Jaya is the Indonesian half of New Guinea, bordering Papua New Guinea to the east.

Bruce didn't mention the idea again until October 1999 when he appeared in London with a ticket to Jakarta in his pocket and announced that he would be standing on the 4,700 meters summit of Gunung Mandala as the sun rose on 1 January 2000. Not only that, he was going to cross the island from south to north at its widest point, using only traditional means of transport on a journey of almost eight hundred miles. After two years in London, a labyrinth of dark valleys covered in malaria-infested jungle sounded to me like paradise. I hadn't been on a serious trip abroad for ages and my fledgling travel company hardly looked as if it was going to help out on that score for at least as long again.

His plan, Bruce told me, was to film the trip if a production company could be persuaded to back the project, but if not he would go anyway. He had a contact in the film industry and now needed to put together a written plan. His non-refundable flight was less than two months away. 'The word so far is that I should take someone else along for filming purposes. Would you be interested?'

Surprise, amazement, elation and panic swept through me, and my mind raced through the implications for Maverick Travel Limited. It had been going for two years but I had run out of capital and was spending much of each week restoring bathtubs with an angle grinder in order to meet the overheads. Every spare penny went into tedious things like brochures that people were clearly putting straight into the bin.

It had been my dream to make a living from proper expeditions ever since I had led my first military one, through Saudi Arabia's 'Empty Quarter' in 1991. It was something I was good at and enjoyed, which might just make a profit when I had left the services. But the few expeditions I had found myself involved with since then had not been of my own design, their aim had drifted away from the ideals of true exploration and endeavour I had set my heart on. Maverick Travel was all about adventure sports but I had made the transition too early: expedition life was far from being out of my system. 'Bruce,' I said, 'I'd do anything to go. It sounds amazing!'

A week later Bruce had produced, with only marginal help from me, an illustrated proposal for the expedition and sent copies to interested parties. He had spent hours in libraries, bookshops and on the Internet tracking down literature on Irian Jaya, most of which had been out of print for over fifty years. The suspense was torture. Would we get the financial backing? I had tried to prepare myself for disappointment but it had become harder to do so with every passing day. The expedition had the makings of an epic adventure – thick jungle, impenetrable valleys, isolated tribes, an ice-capped equatorial peak perhaps still unclimbed, vast swaths of territory not yet mapped. I was whittling away at Bruce's pile of books and found reference to 'the world's largest swamp', 'one of the wildest, most isolated frontiers on Earth', 'freshwater sharks and the world's largest species of crocodile', and 'no one can say for certain that head-hunting and cannibalism do not still occur in the more remote areas…'. Even more exciting, we found nothing that dealt with much of the specific area we planned to traverse. There was mention only in a geographical overview of the region of one of the four peaks with a permanent ice cap, Gunung Mandala. Outsiders did not seem to go there. Irian Jaya seemed only to attract scientists, missionaries, mountaineers and the most intrepid tourists. The mountaineers went only to Puncak

Jaya, hundreds of miles from our mountain and one of the seven continental summits. The tourists, if they went to the mountainous interior at all, got only as far as the easily accessible Baliem valley. The idea that Gunung Mandala might never have been climbed made the hairs rise on the back of my neck – as did the idea that we would have to spend over a month crossing more than two hundred miles of steaming equatorial swamp, ice axes and crampons strapped to our rucksacks, to get half way to it.

With sponsorship, courtesy of Ginger Television Productions, pretty much in the bag we had six weeks before our flight to Jakarta, and decided to go north, to my parents' home in Scotland where we could also get in some climbing and rope-work practice.

Although I had led several expeditions in the army, none had involved scaling a major mountain. Somewhere I had a certificate, dating from one of the first army courses I endured that declared me a 'top-roping and abseiling supervisor'. I remembered standing at the top of a crag somewhere in Wales, watching a staff sergeant inspect my knots and belays, but I had done virtually nothing since.

Bruce's Royal Marines background and a recent 'roped-access' job in Oman meant that he was more experienced. The more reading we did, though, the more we realised that any ropes we carried would be required more for crossing Irian Jaya's many rivers than for mountain-climbing. The last two books Bruce had found, both written in the early 1960s, finally told us some of what we needed to know.

One, *The Sky Above, the Mud Below*, by Tony Saulnier, told of the first crossing of 'Netherlands New Guinea', as it was then known, by foot from the south-east to the north-east. It had been accompanied by a short film of the same title that had won the 1962 Best Documentary award at the Cannes Film Festival. An internationally financed and staffed expedition, involving eighty-nine porters, dozens of air-drops and taking seven months, it had been 'stalked by death'. They lost two porters, and had had particular difficulty in crossing the rivers that frequently confronted them. Their preferred bridging method was to chop down trees until one both fell in the right direction and was not swept away. It often took several days to get everyone across one. We decided to use grappling hooks and a pulley system.

The second book, *To the Mountains of the Stars*, by G.F. Venema, told us that the mountain had been climbed before. This was disappointing, as all Bruce's enquiries to date - Australian, Dutch and British mountaineering associations included – had drawn a blank on Gunung Mandala. It appeared that a massive expedition had been mounted by the Dutch at about the same time as the one that had been filmed. It had been a very different style of trip. Numerous teams had fanned out across the east of the colony to hack their way through and investigate anything of interest that had been spotted from the air. The yellowing pages told of dozens of helicopter landing sites being cleared prior to research teams going in to weigh the 'natives' and take measurements. Only the two colour-plates showing the summit of Gunung Mandala kept me reading. Eventually I discovered a small sketch map that showed the two-week route that a small team had taken through the jungle and on to the rocky upper reaches of the mountain, and thence to the summit. They were photographed wearing crampons on an ice cap recorded as being 325 feet thick. One description grabbed our attention: when the mountaineers reached the top they peered over the other side into a 'stupendous abyss'.

'That's it then. We're going up the south face.' Bruce announced, jabbing a finger at one of the three maps we had acquired. 'No one's been up that!'

I found two of the three unreadable. Dated 1962, one was made up entirely of black ink on white paper and appeared only to indicate where crags lay. No colours showed where forest turned to alpine scrub; no contour lines illuminated the lie of the land. Apart from the occasional indication of a river, there was nothing to suggest what might lie between the rocky outcrops.

The second map was a sort of painting, dated the same year. On it the valleys were vaguely apparent and it had a useful scale of 1:50,000, but I could see little more than a hastily executed watercolour.

The more conventional air-survey chart showed rivers, forests and mountains. And vast white patches, which covered much of the territory north of the mountain range. Hemmed in by the stark green of endless forest they were marked 'Relief Data Incomplete'. Here and there the blue ink of a river crossed between the known and the unknown. My spine tingled when I looked at those patches: uncharted territory along the equator at the end of the twentieth century.

On one aspect of the expedition we were making absolutely no progress. It did not look as though we were going to find an acceptable way to complete the journey legally. We knew that the major part of our planned route was in a political 'no-go zone', but there seemed a chance, with the right backing and groundwork, that we might gain some form of documentation to keep us out of real trouble. The form in which 'real trouble' might manifest itself was another shady area. Without betraying our true intentions we could find no way to discover how far into the interior of Irian Jaya the Indonesian police operated. Where were the checkpoints and would it be feasible to avoid them? Where there was no police presence, could we expect to find a similarly empowered government-appointed 'head man'? Did the Indonesian Army patrol so far from the Papua New Guinea border, and if so could we also expect to stumble across OPM guerrillas fighting for independence? Only four years previously a handful of Cambridge undergraduates had been taken hostage by the Organisasi Papua Merdeka (Free Papua Movement), sparking a major rescue operation and severe reprisals against the local population.

Also, we would be carrying more camera equipment than tourists would need. Ours was a non-political venture but any other motive for heaving all that kit over a mountain range would be difficult to prove. It might conceivably work in our favour among the OPM but we could expect more than a slap on the wrist from Indonesia's troops. The struggle between Irian Jaya's

Javanese governors and the liberation movement had not become known as the 'Bullets Against Bows and Arrows Confrontation' through any compassion on the part of the army. Without the correct travel permits we would also become illegal immigrants after sixty days. There were friends in Jakarta who might sponsor an extended visa but we could not risk compromising them. One told us that an Indonesian team had also climbed Mandala, in 1996, but that the south face was still untouched. He also said we might get permission if we took a military escort with us. I took no time to discard that possibility: soldiers would alienate us from the indigenous peoples, and they would be able to veto anything we attempted to do. They would also have to be paid and fed.

Once in Jakarta we might be able to purchase a semblance of legality with the proverbial brown envelope but it did not seem worth the risk. This far through the planning stage the prospect of jeopardising our chances frightened me far more than that of getting into trouble later on. In fact, whenever we discussed the worst-case scenarios stemming from a surprise encounter with officialdom the item on top of the agenda was always the 'black box' rather than ourselves. Ninety film cassettes – the reason for the journey, as far as our sponsors were concerned - would be packed within a briefcase-sized, waterproof and bomb-proof black Peli-Case. It had to return to Britain with its cargo intact. The 'black box' had taken on a James Bond-style role of its own and our chief contingency plan revolved around an emergency cache, and subsequent secret collection. By no means the only problem with this was how to find something thrown away in thousands of square miles of thick jungle. Whoever had to search for it would have to know its exact location to within 100 feet. Frequent and regular position fixes, acquired by GPS satellite navigation and recorded on small bits of paper secreted on us, would narrow down the search area to within a square kilometre or so, but this wasn't enough.

We found the answer in a London shop: a specially made radio-transmitter with enough battery power for six months would be glued to the outside of the black box and activated as soon as we entered the jungle. If we ran into trouble our first action would be to throw the box into the undergrowth. If we had to abandon it, an Indonesian jungle expert we knew could be sent in to our last known position with equipment designed to pick up the transmitter's signal. Like a Geiger counter, this thing would apparently beep with increasing frequency the nearer it came to the black box.

The planning phase entered the last five working days before departure and equipment was delivered daily: the latest video camera from Japan, clothing and jungle kit, specially made solar panels to charge batteries and sixty kilos of dehydrated rations among much more. I had almost forgotten about the dangers we might face until, on the day of our departure, I received from my mother a St Christopher hanging from a length of nylon string. 'He will keep you safe,' read the note.

I was taken aback. This was the mother who when I once told her I was going to war – it didn't happen – replied, 'Ooh, that'll be fun!' As I boarded the aeroplane I wondered if the real danger now lay in our having an unexpectedly easy time of it.

2 PORT OUT, STARBOARD HOME

The KT Tatamailau looked like a troop ship as she sailed into the harbour at Benoa on the island of Bali and the colourful mass of humanity crowding her starboard side looked eager to get off. A string of pennants and coloured lightbulbs running from bow to funnel to stern gave her a jolly air if you could ignore the sullen mob waiting on the quay to board.

I had been sitting on the quayside with our kit for over four hours. The only entertainment of the afternoon had been a jovial furniture manufacturer from Bima who had delighted in teaching me phrases he prophesised would ease my passage through every situation his country could offer and furthermore leave in my wake crowds of people laughing at my wit.

The thousand-berth ship had not yet finished its home run from Irian Jaya. This was its penultimate stop before it turned around again at the port of Banyuwangi, about six hours away at the eastern tip of Java. We had spent two weeks in Jakarta and had once more failed to get the right travel permits. Travel by boat was a less conspicuous way of arriving in Irian Jaya with 150 kilograms of equipment, but at short notice we had secured a cabin only for those six hours. It looked as though we might have to spend the six-day journey without a secure store for it.

Around two hundred people had disembarked at Benoa and few new passengers boarded with us, yet the ship was packed. Every square foot of outside deck space, on all levels, was covered with people sitting cross-legged on grass mats, sharing out food and seemingly oblivious of passers-by.

'What are the lower decks like? They've got to be more appealing than this.' I stepped through a sizeable family group who were blocking a companionway.

'Go down and have a look,' was all Bruce said, as we dumped our bags in a second-class cabin and I paid the porters who had helped us board. Bruce had had previous experience of the Pelni Line passenger ships running the length and breadth of the archipelago and was already convinced that we were in for a grim voyage.

There was no need to stay long on deck three. With only hours before the end of their journey most of the incumbents were jostling for a position near the stairs and I was in the way. In dormitory K, mounds of rubbish lay between the hundred or so beds. The smell was stifling. Bruce was right; anywhere on deck would be preferable. In comparison, our plastic cabin was like a suite on the Titanic. But we would be booted out of it as soon as we docked at Banyuwangi.

Just after midnight we rigged up our jungle hammocks, as high as possible under the Perspex roof, covering a 'crew only' area, and lashed our bags to the empty life raft racks below us. Exposed to the elements on two sides our spot was made considerably cosier when we stretched the two 'basha' sheets, nylon awnings, round the outside to keep out wind and rain. They had to be adjusted frequently according to the bearing the ship was following and the direction of the wind - and always in the middle of the night when we had woken soaking and buffeted.

I never did figure out the eating arrangements in the lower decks. Early on in the voyage, we managed to secure tickets to the dining room where the ship's officers mingled with the first and second-class passengers. An American missionary couple and their three young children, the only other Westerners aboard, were returning to the troubled island of Ambon from where they had been forced to flee more than a year previously. They had a meal ticket for each of the eight beds in their two cabins and kindly donated two to us. They also agreed to store some of our equipment for us. Now when the weather was bad we could retreat to the dining room to read and play with our maps, chopping each one down to the relevant areas, waterproofing them, and painstakingly cross-referencing every feature - village, river bend, airstrip - in longitude and latitude. Eventually the air-survey chart showed twice the information it had previously.

We passed a ceaseless parade of islands, the Ring of Fire, on both sides. Occasionally a perfectly symmetrical cone appeared through the rain, thrusting straight from the waves. One island, just off the starboard side, carried an immense lava flow a mile wide and covered in low scrub, sloping gently into the sea from the cloud-topped upper flanks. We dropped anchor at several isolated ports, a few in daylight; brightly coloured fishing communities nestled in the green embrace of dormant giants from which small boats sailed out to the Tatamailau, offering fresh fruit and dried fish for sale until the ship's whistle announced departure.

At Ambon we took over one of the missionary family's cabins. Finally, in the early hours of the seventh day, we arrived at Timika and the end of this leg of our journey. I went on deck for a look. I knew the town was twenty miles up a river but I had never expected the scene that emerged as my eyes grew accustomed to the dark.

We were anchored in the river, nose to current. On either side, not more than eighty or so metres away, a solid wall of jungle loomed out of the darkness, its presence betrayed only by the glow from the Tatamailau's light bulbs. We had docked in the middle of a wood, and the scene could not have been more surreal. The ship seemed to have become a solitary island of light, a last fortress against the inhospitable forest. Even the air smelt different: no longer the clean sea breeze, it was still, damp, potent, thick.

Accompanied by the rattle of small, single-cylinder engines running to different beats, dim lights approaching from upstream were extinguished one by one as the boats carrying them entered our orb. There was one large *klotok,* a traditional Indonesian fishing boat, several smaller ones, and a similar number of long, slim, canoe-like craft powered by outboards. The big *klotok* was packed beyond belief. Even the wheelhouse was generating money, supporting a mass of people, its windows half-obscured by the dangling legs of those sitting around the edge. Very gingerly it manoeuvred alongside whilst the smaller boats circled like the 'little ships' of Dunkirk around a destroyer. The air was full of shouts and the clatter of diesels.

For this one scene alone the last six days had been worthwhile.

The porters who came aboard to help carry baggage were Irianese. Tall and bigger-boned, they were lean and strong. Their heavy brows, wild hair and wide eyes, set deep in dark skin, gave them an almost threatening appearance but they were quick to laugh. No one paid the slightest attention to Bruce and me. This forest was home to these men, and not to the Indonesians on board. We were no longer the only foreigners.

We waited for the scrum to subside before climbing with our baggage into a longboat with about ten others and their possessions. Sitting in the bow I looked back at the ship, her festive lights a challenge to the forest - and I thought of Joseph Conrad's *Heart of Darkness*. Then we were curving into the first bend and the scene had gone. It was utterly dark.

A man squatting on the prow found the way ahead with a weak torch but we had only motored around the first few bends when other lights appeared. Three stilted huts sat in the water on the left side of the current, so close together they looked joined at the hip.

'*Ma'af Inggris bapak,*' Excuse me English sirs, our driver called forward to us over the heads of the other passengers, '*Polis!*'

I didn't feel ready for the police.

Other boats chuntered past up the river as we slowed down and our fellow passengers groaned at the delay.

'Let me do the talking,' Bruce said quietly as we pulled alongside a dugout canoe tied up to the stilts. 'We should be all right here but you never know - and your Indonesian isn't good enough yet.'

Two Javanese policemen squatted on the edge of the platform, one of them repeatedly switching his torch beam from Bruce's face to mine, then back again, until all I could see were spots.

'Leave them alone!' a woman in the back of our boat shouted, and everyone on board laughed. The policemen smiled and shrugged. They were only as officious as bored policemen tend to be and despite slitting open the plastic food bags in the course of their search – for drugs apparently - asked easily fended questions.

Our papers, and the torch they had borrowed to check them, were returned and we went on our way.

But for the noise of the outboard engine the next hour could not have been more atmospheric. There was hardly any light. The edges of the river appeared suddenly as a high wall towering over us. Whenever we glimpsed it we were only seconds from impact. A shout from the lookout and the engine was cut, the boat lurching as our wake swept underneath it, everyone holding their breath, waiting for the crunch. Then we would move forward again as the driver found his bearings. I lent the bow lookout my torch and progress became faster.

Every so often a spectral tree would appear ahead, lighting the way with a flickering, ethereal glow, like a ghostly Christmas decoration floating in the air. The first of these had me utterly mystified until we passed it and I saw that thousands of fireflies had gathered among its leaves in a luminous orgy of phosphorescence.

As we entered the second hour the bow look-out, very drunk on an opaque liquid he was swigging from a Fanta bottle, was bellowing incomprehensibly into my right ear. He commanded my attention, even when I lay slumped against the gunwale feigning exhausted sleep. I could understand few words but got the gist of his rhetoric quickly. It was a political tirade against his Javanese rulers. The Javanese man next to Bruce was laughing.

Timika owes its existence as a town to Freeport Mine, the largest opencast copper mine in the world, lying among the mountains to the north. Typical of a service town, its grid layout, cheap, concrete buildings and wide, dusty streets are uninspiring. Its only asset for the casual visitor is a much-praised Sheraton Hotel, all polished teak. We checked in as the sun came up over tropical gardens and a complicated swimming pool. It was Bruce's idea - I would never have considered it: I was all set for the cheap and dismal. Bruce pointed out that it was our last chance to live it up a little. 'We'll be sleeping in a bubbling swamp from now on, living off maggots pulled from our own wounds!' he averred.

We had little to do in Timika except hire a boat to take us down the coast and pick up the cash we would need for the expedition. In his book *I Came From the Stone Age*, Heinrich Harrer, the man who first climbed Puncak Jaya in the 1960s, had paid his porters with cowrie shells collected in Hawaii. The sackloads of obvious wealth had been a constant worry and it looked as though we faced the same problem. Stupidly we failed to take bags to the bank and had to stagger back along the street laden with several thousand pounds' worth of notes ranging from the equivalent of twenty pence to a pound, the only denominations of any use in small villages. There were enough to fill a large wheelbarrow. Fortunately the shifty-looking crowd of men who watched us were too stunned to think of robbing us and we fell into a taxi convulsed with laughter. The driver knew a man with a speedboat.

Back in the air-conditioned opulence of the Sheraton we had a bottle of Margaux with supper. The cutlery reminded me that I still lacked one of the most important items of equipment a man can carry into the field. From the way he went on about it, Bruce's spoon, an old favourite from previous expeditions, must have had mystical qualities. I pocketed a Sheraton one.

3 THE SEASON OF THE WAVES

The speedboat was a disarmingly small four-seater, entirely inadequate for the two of us, two drivers, our baggage and what was apparently the season of the waves. However, once out of the forest and into open sea, the water was almost flat and we made good speed. They would be able to return tomorrow, the driver told us, but after that - he swept his arm across the southern horizon and rolled his eyes horribly - '*Matti!*' Dead!

It's no wonder the waves can be big in that area: the whole journey was across shallows. At least half a dozen times, when the shoreline was but a distant line of trees appearing to hover just above the shimmering horizon, like a mirage, the men had to jump out and push. Whenever the boat stopped and the rush of air ceased, the heat bore down on me with startling ferocity. I could barely talk. Light relief came once, in the form of a flying fish demonstrating a singular lack of skill in the air by slamming into the side of my head, but it was altogether a brief laugh and our arrival at Agats was like reaching a desert oasis. I began to realise that I was ill.

Agats is an unusual place. Built entirely on stilts over the black mud of the south bank of the Aswetsj river where it meets the sea, its pavements are raised wooden walkways while 'roads' exist only at high tide when the river comes rushing in to fill narrow culverts and drains, turning them into navigable waterways. It was low tide when we tied up against the riverside edge of town, and a full fifteen feet up a makeshift ladder to Yeodi's 'back yard'. Yeodi, in common with many of the traders and business-owners in Agats, was a Bugi, from South Sulawesi. He and two small boys helped us drag everything up and his wife left her baking to watch us. The main street was on the other side of their impressive house. Here planks covered the entire area – about twenty feet wide - between the rows of shops and houses, while elsewhere in the town a drop in the mud flanked the narrow walkways.

Yeodi showed us to his cousin's place, the Spartan but adequate Asmat Inn. Our arrival was met with good-natured derision from a group of ribald women selling vegetables and fruit on the boardwalk in front of it. Bruce bought a bunch of enormous bananas. Inside, the inn was dark and cool, its eight identical rooms off an airy lounge. They were the usual budget fare - two beds, a small table, broken fan, and an en-suite bathroom complete with a tap and bucket. The loo in each was merely a hole in the floor, flushed twice a day by the tide.

Agats is the administrative capital, the commercial, educational and communications hub of the Asmat region, and the local headquarters of the Catholic mission since 1953. It was also the starting point of our expedition. There was nothing left in our way now but registration with the local authorities – already alerted to our presence - and the purchase of a suitable canoe. With the clock already ticking on our visas and permits neither of us wished to hang around. We found the chief of police just past the helicopter-landing pad where over forty barefoot youths were playing football on the roughly-hewn planks. He was relaxed and affable, chatting in Indonesian for a while before we got to the point.

'Perhaps we will go to Senggo,' Bruce lied.

'Ah, yes. All tourists go to Senggo. You can fly out to Merauke from there.' And that was it: our permits were stamped without further preamble, and without suspicion of our true intentions.

That evening, at the Asmat Museum of Culture and Progress, I had to sit down suddenly next to a display of daggers made from human femurs – I felt awful, unable to give much attention to the fantastic collection of carvings, weaponry, shields, trophy skulls, ritual costumes, bird-of-paradise feather head dresses and terrifying masks that surrounded me. For the next three days I fought off some unknown fever. Prudence demanded that Bruce treat me for malaria, which he did, but neither of us was convinced that that was what it was.

A day through my illness a softly-spoken man called Harun introduced himself as a river guide and possible purveyor of a canoe and paddles. He announced this in faltering English, and his knowledge of the Siretsj river and, more importantly, whom we might meet along its banks convinced us that he was our man - at least for the time being. Outside my door, he and Bruce pored over the maps.

Initially we had planned to make it to Atsj (pronounced A-tch') before we bought the canoe and slipped quietly away. Agats was on the wrong river but a short boat ride round the coast would bring us to the mouth of the one we wanted, the Siretsj. Atsj, a logging settlement, lay on the west bank just a few miles upstream and would, we thought, be a more discreet place to set out from. Every recent account of travelling by boat through the Asmat that we had read, mentioned a police escort, which we were desperate to avoid. In any case, if we bought the canoe in Agats we would have to paddle round the coast in the season of the waves, which seemed unwise.

Wrong, said Harun, there was a shortcut through the swamp. Everyone used it. 'But there are many different ways,' he mumbled. 'You will need me to show you the right one.'

'What about the police? What will they say?'

'People will think it is strange, but you are tourists. There was a German man some years ago who canoed by himself to Senggo. He spent many days practising first. Nobody stopped him.'

There is little to choose between Asmat canoes, at least to the uninitiated. The vast majority are straightforward dugouts, differing only in size and age. Two possibilities lay in the mud at Sjuru, a village just fifteen minutes of boardwalk away, and we opted for the larger. At seven metres long it seemed gigantic, but when I envisaged our baggage stowed amidships I could see it almost too short. We christened our craft *Wandy*, after Wandy Swales, an adventurer in the classic mould whose expeditions had introduced us to Indonesia.

The following day my temperature had dropped and the canoe

was ready for us. Harun had burnt palm fronds beneath it to close the pores in the wood, then scraped off the charred bits. We would leave tomorrow. We were on the threshold of a journey beyond one of the 'last frontiers' to a land that had remained dark and hidden for longer than almost any other. Whatever we had read or been told, I was confident that we would find something extraordinary - I had read of tricky encounters with fierce and murderous tribesmen as recently as the late eighties.

'I can't go tomorrow,' said Harun, looking down at the floor. 'It's Christmas – my wife won't let me.'

We stared at him incredulously. We hadn't considered this possibility.

'I can only leave on the twenty-seventh.'

To make amends Harun offered to take us to some of the *bisjmam* villages that lay along this one stretch of the coastal region. The most prized examples of the Asmat's famous ancestor poles, or *bisj*, were made there and nowhere else. Bruce went with him but I stayed behind. I knew that these were the most visited of all the Asmat villages and I needed to recover my strength.

Captain Cook was the first European to have a go at entering the Asmat when he stopped for water in 1770 in what is now Cook's Bay, a little south of Agats. One report has it that he and two officers got barely two hundred yards before being met with puffs of lime and a shower of arrows from the tree-line. They were chased back to the ship by around a hundred Asmat in war canoes and full rig. Nobody knows when the Asmat first settled the area but there is evidence, through studies in blood typing and artwork, that they are related to the island's other famous woodcarvers, the Sepik of north Papua New Guinea. If that is so perhaps they perhaps crossed the mountains to occupy the southern swamplands just a few hundred years before they saw Cook.

Over the centuries following Cook's retreat, a handful of other explorers reported on the hostility of the area, but the Asmat were left pretty much alone until 1925 when the colonial Dutch set up a post just to the north, in the neighbouring territory of the Mimikan, who were enemies, and targets for head-hunting raids. In 1930 the Mimikan and the Dutch police ambushed an Asmat raiding party of 400 men and slaughtered all but sixteen. The survivors were marched off to jail. The outside world had arrived.

On Christmas Day we went to church joining a stream of smartly-dressed worshippers filing along the boardwalks towards the cathedral. The building deserved the distinction. It was an impressive open-sided structure with a lofty, angular tin roof atop a skeleton of local redwood and could have seated a thousand with room to spare. A cool breeze wafted through the congregation and out again over the high-tide that rose and fell silently beneath the polished wooden floor. The Catholic service, conducted by the Bishop of Agats from a pulpit flanked by a black Madonna, was delivered in Asmat and I could only join in with 'Amen'. Distant walkways across the encircling water and overhanging greenery glowing translucently in the sun gave me the impression that I was in a large Japanese water garden, perhaps attending a Shinto ceremony. It seemed so far removed from the Christmas Day services of my childhood, which had to compete with presents, television, and oven-timings. Up and down the rivers, Asmat villages of a mere 200 people would be fielding larger congregations than that less than fifty years after the first missionary had risked life and limb to spread the word among a flock who were busy eating each other. It was a remarkable achievement from any standpoint.

The first missionaries arrived in Western New Guinea over 150 years ago - Dutch Protestants. In those early days more of them died from malaria than there were converts made, but by the beginning of the twentieth century Catholic and Protestant missionaries were flooding in. In 1912 the Dutch colonial authorities decreed that the Protestants should have the north, the Catholics the south; and while this arrangement was shelved in 1955 the Catholic Church still dominates the south and there are more Protestants in the north. By the 1950s Christianity had reached the less accessible inland regions.

There was a marked difference in the methods of Catholics and Protestants. The Protestant missionaries set about tearing down the fabric of the communities they came across, determined that the people should eschew everything in their lives and customs that was morally and biblically indefensible. The Catholics followed a more benign, pragmatic approach. Of course, there was quite a lot going on that had to be stopped - such as headhunting and wife-swapping - but there was much to be built upon. The rituals and beliefs of the Irianese, they realised, were vital to the stability and spiritual health of each community. They should therefore not only be encouraged but, where possible, adapted to Christianity - the cathedral I was sitting in had been inaugurated in the same manner as a longhouse, the political and spiritual hub of the village. The Catholic fathers and brothers saw that their first duty, before saving souls, was to attend to the earthly welfare of the people around them. They administered medicine and became the tribes-people's only representatives before the Indonesian authorities - saving lives, and risking their own to do so.

Among the congregation in front of me there was a tall man with straight, greying hair and white skin, the only other Westerner I could see in the cathedral. Afterwards he introduced himself in a soft American accent, as Father Virgil, the head of the Crosier mission in Agats, and invited us for a cup of tea at 'mission control'. There was a natural serenity in every movement Father Virgil made. I suddenly remembered I had read of a Brother Virgil in Agats who had 'appeared, floating ethereally over the gleaming floor towards us'. It had to be the same man. The book, *Skullduggery* by Mark Shand, had been published in 1987 and he told us that he had been there since 1981.

Bruce asked him what chances we had of encountering uncontacted peoples along our route to the mountains.

'I haven't heard of a new contact for some years,' he said, 'but that doesn't mean there aren't any more out there. There's a lot of ground upriver we haven't got to.'

4 THE LAND OF EX-HEADHUNTERS

With Christmas and Boxing Day out of the way we could finally get underway. As Harun had requested the night before, Bruce and I had all the equipment stacked on the jetty at Sjuru in time for low tide at six thirty. A large crowd was gathering as I leapt into the canoe to take charge of stowage.

As Sjuru and Agats receded behind us I made myself comfortable on the forward food bag, braced my feet against the rucksack in front and dipped my paddle into the water. Thank God we had gone for the larger of the two canoes. As it was there was only just enough room between the bags for us to put our feet. Behind me, Bruce was already powering away from his seat in the middle. Harun stood easily in the pointed stern, both steering and powering with each stroke. Our dugout cut through the water smoothly, only the paddles breaking that first silence with a rhythmic plop. We had been enveloped in cacophony since arriving in Indonesia. Now it was suddenly quiet. I concentrated on my stroke, aware that Bruce and Harun were now synchronising theirs with mine.

Carved from a single piece of redwood, the Asmat paddles had slender blades and tremendously long shafts of around eight feet. They had to be long enough for a standing man to paddle with, of course, but the fine points and occasional barbs seemed to hint at a second, more sinister purpose, a relic of the days when war canoes would hurtle up river, silently powered by nine or more naked painted warriors on their way to harvest a fresh crop of heads. Traditionally, though, the paddle-ends were more likely to have sported the carved face of a slain relative on their handles, acting as a daily reminder of retribution yet to be carried out.

Another dugout came out of the forest ahead, powered by

father and son standing at each end. Between them, among scattered papaya, and manioc leaves, squatted mum with two girls, their eyes averted. In chorus we hailed them in Asmat just before Harun, bristling with pride, rattled off a full explanation. The womenfolk could no longer resist a glance and were at once riveted. Conscious of the damage this must be doing to her daughters, mum, without averting her gaze from us, held an ineffective arm vaguely in front of their eyes. Harun and the man conversed with each other until almost a hundred metres separated the two craft. Then, suddenly, the sun was off us and the jungle closed overhead.

We were following a definite waterway but the absence of a discernible bank and Harun's careful navigation around the many trees sticking out of the water, gave the impression that we had lost the way and simply plunged into the swamp. Only a thickening of growth on either side marked the boundaries of our river. Although it was barely past seven o'clock, steam curled from the surface and hung in the air, exposing sharply any sunlight penetrating the canopy above but also softening the colour contrasts; green against brown against green. Our bow wave sent silent ripples through the slick of forest ooze matting the water on either side, while trailing from an occasional stick, the faintest of wakes indicated the current that had cleared our passage through the slime, a dark gloss breach like an open lead through polar ice.

It was noisy in there, though. Our own silent, and inconspicuous progress made no interruption to the shrill, feathered ruckus going on in the branches above. Hidden flocks were too busy chattering among themselves to notice our arrival until the last minute when they would scatter loudly. My untrained eyes caught only fleeting glimpses of the odd retreat and never the flashing colours I imagined adorning the owners of those fantastic calls. Irian Jaya is home to the greatest and most spectacular array of birds-of-paradise in the world but it was sadly apparent that we would be lucky even to see them clearly, let alone catch any on film.

At intervals we would pass shadowy creeks where the surface scum snaked away into the trees. Vigilantly we scanned these sinister inlets for crocodiles - the ones that live in the Asmat swamps and rivers are estuarine, or 'salties', the biggest reptiles in the world. None appeared here, though, and we might not have bothered looking at all had we met the second group of locals earlier than we did. Four young men were manoeuvring a raft of three very large redwood logs towards us through the shadows. One squatted amidships whilst only the heads of his colleagues showed above the dark water. The attitude of each head showed that some sub-aquatic struggle was taking place, but whether their wood was caught on a submerged branch, or tangled in the roots of the overhanging vegetation they didn't seem in any desperate hurry to leave the water. I asked Harun about man-eating monsters.

'*Semua matti*, all dead - they are all hunted,' he informed us. I had been told that much of the crocodile hunting along Irian Jaya's south coast had been sponsored by the then chief of nature conservation, who happened to own a shoe factory, but as with most of my information, this was ten years old and unconfirmed.

At about midday we emerged from a hole in the green wall, into daylight and a much wider waterway, the Jet river. It began to rain, gently at first, but increasing in strength until we were paddling through a grey blanket. Two huts appeared straight in front of us, near the bank but seemingly not attached to it. One was clearly tumbledown and the grass eaves of the other hung so low as to touch the water that all but obscured its stilts. Harun parked our log under the floor and the three of us piled inside for lunch.

By mid afternoon my arms, shoulders and back had nothing left in them. Whatever exercise I had done to prepare for this - I could not recall having done any - had not been enough. I hoped that at least it looked from behind as if I was pulling my weight because it didn't feel as though I was. Each successive paddle stroke was feebler as we crept along the left-hand bank, hugging the side to avoid the tidal current. The only indication I had that Bruce might also be tiring was the increasing number of paddle clashes as we lost, and fought to regain, the rhythm.

I rejoiced silently when the village of Warse appeared ahead of us, its forty or so huts and huge longhouse straddling the junction of the Jet and the Powet rivers. By the time we actually arrived in the little marina of dugouts along the muddy bank, however, there had been ample time for even the oldest citizen to make it down to the river.

A crowd of perhaps fifty Asmatters awaited us at the top of a treacherous-looking slope, women in ragged skirts and T-shirts, men in shorts. As our greeting was returned one man leapt down on to a half-buried palm log and held the bow for us while others stood by to prevent us falling into the slimy, paint-like grey mud. I slipped off the palm log despite two helping hands. But there wasn't the tittering I had expected: the murmur of concern sounded more like self-admonishment for not having a visitor-friendly jetty.

Warse's longhouse looked as if it had been rebuilt recently. It could not have been much less than two hundred feet long, sporting thirteen front doors and thirteen back doors, thirteen fireplaces, and a system of steps impossible for Westerners to surmount with heavy loads. My rucksack was plucked from my shoulder with little sign of effort by a young man who sprang up the remaining slippery poles and disappeared inside. Our hosts were a muscular lot. Even those who looked well into their sixties and beyond were taut-skinned and powerful.

'Human flesh must be packed full of protein,' Bruce remarked. 'Some of these men are probably old enough, and look at them!'

I had to agree. Much of the literature on the Asmat dwelt at length on their cannibalistic and head-hunting practices, and isolated instances had been reported as late as the 1980s.

A roll of drum beats, rising to a crescendo then ending suddenly with a synchronised shout, welcomed us as we stepped into the cool shade beneath the palm leaf roof. Up against each of the thirteen pillars supporting the long roof was a carved and painted ancestor pole, ten feet high and a foot wide, reminiscent of the totems of the North American Indians. Grotesque heads crowned tiny foetal bodies, one on top of the other, eyes glaring from stark white faces.

Two of the drummers leapt to their feet and pulled down from the rafters a reed mat that was ceremoniously laid out for us in front of a man sitting with his back against the central roof support. He wasn't the only one to be wearing a fine hat of yellow *cuscus* fur adorned with white feather plumes but his bearing and position within the longhouse left me in no doubt that this was the *kepala desa*, or chief. We shook his hand and offered him a fresh bag of tobacco, which he accepted with a curt nod before motioning us to sit. Then the men and boys who had led us in closed around us in a wide circle. Harun told our story and all eyes were soon on the two intriguing-looking boxes, black and orange. Everyone wanted to see themselves on film so we went through what was to become a ritual of our journey: filming them while simultaneously showing them their faces on the side screen.

The nine men sitting cross-legged before us now picked up their carved wooden drums again and began beating out a steady rhythm while six more jumped up and began warming their own instruments over the embers of the fire, tightening the stretched lizard skins for a desired note. The rest of the crowd spread out through the building, dancing to the drums, while a mournful chant emanated from five of the men in the circle. Each dancer was rooted to the spot, upper body, arms and head still, while the knees were thrust sideways at each drum beat. Many appeared almost to be in a state of trance, staring vacantly ahead, while an unselfconscious fluidity permeated the simple movement.

Soaking up the scene, I noticed that each of the thirteen doorways facing away from the river towards the rest of the village framed a crowd of faces, all peering in at us. Harun followed my gaze. 'Women and children only allowed in *jeu* (longhouse) for special occasions,' he said.

Harun told us he would come no further with us. He hated

paddling. He would arrange for a man to take us to Amborep, the next village, he told us, where we would find another guide, called Premus. Amborep was on the junction with the Siretsj, just four hours away.

I was sorry to lose him but it was an opportunity to employ a stronger arm at the stern, perhaps even two.

The *kepala desa* of Warse took us on a tour of the village, with the village population in tow. My Indonesian was not up to the spiel on what was what so I strode ahead to film the processional advance. Joined together by a sturdy walkway above the mud, the place was deceptively large. A tin roof covered the church-cum-school but the remainder of the buildings were traditionally built family houses of two rooms, the kitchen and living space. It would not be popular for us to enter one of these, Harun told us, nipping an impending faux-pas in the bud. Strange men were entertained in the longhouse, lest they are tempted to steal someone's wife. Bruce's sceptical expression matched my own. There were no beauties here.

Back in the longhouse I raised the subject of food. Until now we had been eating Indonesian fare. I was keen to try an Asmat supper. I asked a man if we could buy *sago* or something, fish perhaps, fruits of the forest, but was surprised to learn that the village had no food to sell us at all. As rural villages go, Warse did not look as if it was at the bottom of the economic ladder. Yes, these were poor people - hunters, gatherers and primitive horticulturists with less than ideal land for anything but *sago*, taro and various obscure fruits - but the village was well kept and everyone looked extremely healthy.

'Sorry, Mr Mark. He says they do not want to sell any food,' said Harun after I had asked a second time, unsure if the men had understood me. I was about to ask why this was, but something in his manner told me not to push the matter any further, as if it was of grave embarrassment to our hosts.

'Well, I'm starving. Let's try some of our own food.' I thought of the five different menus we had in the red bags.

'If we have to eat our own stuff from day one we'll never

get over the mountains, let alone across the island,' said Bruce. 'And if we cook on these boys' fire what will it look like if we don't offer them all a taste?' He was right, but I was still starving. Eventually he capitulated. In the event, the vegetarian casserole was delicious. The *kepala desa* loved it too.

I awoke the following morning spectacularly uncomfortable, and cold, the bamboo slats of the floor embedded in my arm. Somehow I had managed to fall asleep both outside the mosquito net we had intended to share and at least six feet away from the reed matting our hosts had laid down for us. My roll-mat was still attached to my rucksack. The sun was not yet above the forest canopy and a grey, dirty light crept through the doorways like a mist. The floor down the middle of the longhouse seemed to be coming alive; writhing like a tangle of vipers under a black sheet were forms I couldn't make out. Grunting and yawning, the shadowy morass began to morph into human forms as, in a startling rush, men sat up all over the hut, as if a huge alarm clock had gone off. They all looked in my direction, as if to check we were still there, then went back to more stretching and yawning. It was light very quickly.

Our two new paddlers were dour and unresponsive. Their scorn at our clumsy, seated efforts was almost tangible. I envied them their ability to stand up in this precarious craft. No doubt the paddling was easier when you could put your whole body behind each stroke but it was also more graceful and in tune with both the ethos of a dugout canoe and the environment we were in.

Arriving in Amborep at midday we learnt that Premus, our possible new guide, had gone fishing and would not return until the evening.

There wasn't a great deal to do. I wandered about inside the *jeu*, examining the bundles of bows and arrows stuck for safe keeping behind the rattan ties that bound sections of wall together. Some of the arrows, of bamboo or wood, were tipped with roughly shaped and beaten steel bound in place with string smeared in pig's fat. One had been made from a teaspoon, hammered flat and ground to a point. I scanned the rafters for things of interest: the carved and painted war shields or *jamasj* perhaps, whose stylistic designs had been considered so terrifying that a warrior, given the choice, would more readily go into battle carrying one rather than a spear, axe or bow. Perhaps there might be some stone axes.

'They have all been sold,' said an old man, with an enormous coil of white clamshell, half an inch wide, drooping from either side of his nose. His eyes held mine; there was a sadness in them that hadn't been in his voice. Bruce was still examining the arrows. An old hand at stringing a bow with rattan string, he demonstrated for the camera and set an arrow in place for firing. There was a shout of alarm from the old man, then everyone else in the longhouse sprang back a few paces, ducking and covering their heads with their arms. The old man, with no trace of anger, removed the arrow. Bruce's apology was met with a gale of laughter.

'No weapons are carried inside the *jeu*.' A young man grinned broadly at us. 'It is our custom. The *jeu* is a place for talking.'

As in the *jeu* at Warse, there was a long row of ancestor poles, but here they supported the roof. Though crude and basic in comparison to those we had seen in the Agats museum, they had also been whittled from a buttress-rooted tree. The top figure on each pole sported a huge erect phallus, in the crook of which sat a central beam running the length of the building.

Another delay so early in our journey was irksome. Sitting under the eaves of the longhouse Bruce and I contemplated setting off on our own. The tide would turn soon so we would have the right current once we were on the Siretsj itself. We could canoe through the night until the next ebb, then camp on the bank. At least there weren't many crocodiles around these days.

'Let's look at that in more detail shall we?' I ventured. Bruce appeared to have forgotten the 'sea-trials' we had conducted in *Wandy* on Boxing Day when he had not managed to steer the thing in a straight line at all. I had, but at the expense of any forward propulsion that might have come from my paddle.

'Steering's a problem.'

'We'll get better at it.'

'I'll get better at it you mean. You'll be doing the powering. The tide should help, though. We could just drift if need be.'

'We won't be able to see logs and stuff in the dark until it's too late.'

We sat in silent thought for a while.

'But it would be a laugh,' Bruce said.

I considered the proposition. We had never planned to have anyone helping us in the first place and further upriver we might find ourselves canoeing after dark just to get past the police.

'We could probably sleep in the canoe if we tied up inside one of those little creeks,' Bruce went on. 'The only bummer with the whole idea is that we will have used up a set of batteries.'

'There might be a moon and we've got enough. Let's go for it.'

'Let's give Premus until five o'clock then load the canoe.' Bruce had wound up the discussion.

I went back to my book. An Asmat warrior required at least three heads for a successful and glorious journey through life: his own, and two more hacked from the shoulders of his enemies. The first of the latter pair would have been harvested by his father in time for his birth. Then, if he was lucky enough to reach his teens, he would complete his transition from boy to man by taking the head of an enemy warrior so that he would inherit the dead man's strength and valour, wisdom and potency. The young warrior might also feast on other parts of his victim likely to imbue him with spiritual wealth. Father André Dupeyrat, a catholic missionary in New Guinea during the thirties and forties, recalled how one of his flock explained the fate of Dzaboutai, a widely renowned war chief of an enemy tribe, whose head he now held in his hands. 'I gave my two sons - they will one day become chiefs - his eyes to eat. To my wife I gave his sexual organs. To my warriors, I gave the heart, the liver and the entrails, so that they should become fearless. As for me, by this hole you see here, I sucked out Dzaboutai's brains, and I keep his skull in honour, for his valour has entered into me.'

Strangely, the young warrior might take over the family relationships of the murdered man. He would be welcomed into his victim's home like a long-lost child, symbolically invited to suckle at the matriarch's breast. Because of this custom, warring villages often went through periods of peaceful interaction.

'*Selamat! Nama saya Premus*'. A middle-aged man in shorts and T-shirt was standing over us. It was Premus.

Premus had already been told what we were doing and took charge immediately. He had brought his son along to paddle us to his house. We would stay there overnight and leave as the tide turned just before dawn. He pointed out his home, a solitary hut on the opposite bank, on the confluence of the Powet and the Siretsj. We warmed to him immediately. His eyes shone with enthusiasm and he was proud to have been sought out as a river guide. What position he had held, if any, in the village up until this moment was unclear but now he barked out orders to a group of loiterers and, in a trice, *Wandy* was packed and ready.

Inside the house it was pitch dark until I offered a candle. We were in a largish room with a central pole supporting the palm-leaf roof. Mrs Premus was through a doorway at the back, preparing to cook. As we sat down, cross-legged, on the floor, another two boys and a little girl appeared, an attentive audience for our saga. I was becoming better at explaining what we were doing there but it was trickier to describe why we wanted to do it. We were not there to buy carvings, and could not risk disclosing our aim to climb Gunung Mandala and cross the island.

Premus liked the idea of paddling upriver rather than motoring - I liked him for that alone. He appreciated the aesthetics of the traditional way and only wanted to be sure that we understood how long it would take.

'Do you think his children are strong enough to paddle us?' I wondered aloud.

The oldest boy, Agus, was in his teens and looked strong enough, so we suggested it. An almost carnival atmosphere evolved: this was going to net the Premus family a useful wad of cash.

The deal was done. However, canoes, river and money swiftly exhausted our vocabulary. It was the very situation for which we had brought an inflatable globe. I rummaged around in the gift bag for it. We chose easily interpretable facts: New Guinea is the second largest island in the world, Greenland is No 1; in Greenland at the moment there is no sun but in six months' time there will be no darkness. Irian Jaya has a million people; Greater London has 15 million people. In Scotland it rains ice everywhere so it is this deep on the ground (wildly exaggerated) and very cold. If a man urinates outside, in five minutes it will have turned to ice. Premus translated the Indonesian into Asmat, keeping up with the barrage of astonishing information. Each cry of amazement spurred us on to greater, more lavish embellishments until our audience could take no more.

The next morning *Wandy* had all but sunk into the mud under a tropical deluge and looked like an immovable cattle trough. Had the tide turned yet? The river looked viscous and slow in the first glow of dawn, like crude oil. I wanted to lie back and watch the changing light, lulled into a gently rocking slumber by the work of others. It had been a horrible night, sleep denied me by clouds of *agas* flies, identical in size and disposition to the 'midges' of Scotland's north-west.

By the time we were loaded and under way, settling into the rhythm set by Premus on the bow, the sky was lightening. The figure before me, paddling with such fluidity that he appeared to be part of the canoe, sharpened from vague outline into stark silhouette, the point of his paddle tracing a ceaseless ellipse against the dawn. Approaching Premus's house the previous evening I hadn't taken in how big this river was. Now I could hardly drag my eyes from its immensity: it was at least a quarter of a mile wide.

We paddled in silence, keeping within fifteen feet of the left bank and in the glow of the rising sun. Deep in shadow, the right bank looked so far away as to be part of another land. Motionless egrets marked the numerous floating logs and trees, slender white spearmen against the black backdrop, like sentinel spirits silently guarding the darkness. We heard the thundering wing beat of passing hornbills and the plop of lazy fish. Once or twice the plop was more of a splash and accompanied by movement in the undergrowth but it was just big fish panicking. We could have been a thousand miles from anywhere, four men in a log.

The village of Fos crept into view mid-afternoon as we rounded a sweeping bend. At first sight, even from afar, it did not bode well for the purchase of food. The *jeu* and surrounding huts were despondent and decomposing, the colour of rotting hay. The people looked no different from those we had met before but I noticed a higher incidence of yaws - an unpleasant-looking skin condition that was common until penicillin reached these parts. In the *jeu* the welcoming drum ceremony was unchanged but plain poles supported the roof and the floor was riven with holes. No mats were rolled up in the rafters and none were offered; there was an aura of decline. I hadn't known exactly what to expect because everything I had read was ten years out of date, but an hour before we reached Fos there had been a sign that perhaps nothing had changed in that time.

We had passed piles of redwood trunks waiting to be floated down river. I had read about logging companies, exploiting local populations as slaves while they destroyed the forest on which those people had to subsist. Usually paid nothing, Asmat villagers were savagely beaten and even killed by the police for not fulfilling the monthly felling quotas forced on them, and there was evidence that the corruption stretched back to the highest echelons of government. Forced into the forest for long periods they had little time to gather food and attend to the upkeep of their homes. As the ironwood trees were removed, many of the existing *sago* palms on which the people depended were either destroyed or left without the shade they needed to survive. In the late 1960s United Nations observers had found a virtual holocaust going on here. The most recent of our books, the 1990 *Periplus Guide to Irian Jaya*, by Kal Muller, claimed this practice had ceased in the early 1980s, but I wasn't convinced.

Another book, *Poisoned Arrows*, by George Monbiot, written just a year earlier in 1989, gave evidence that suggested that timber slavery was still going at the time of writing. Even if it had been stopped now, the people were still next to the same shattered forest. They might have time to find food, but if *sago* was still in short supply that might explain there was no time to repair the village. Viewed from the river, the forest looked fine, but most of the timber growing in the Asmat is commercially unviable so it was never going to be felled. I knew from several sources that the ironwood had been cleared out of these downstream areas long ago.

So, what about the piles of logs we had seen? Was that being cut by the locals for their own purposes, or were the authorities now clearing out the redwood? Were the people still being exploited as a labour source, or were they simply engaged full time in just feeding themselves because the forest had gone into the pockets of a few Javanese?

As the drums were put aside I fished out a fresh bag of rolling tobacco and packet of papers, offering them to the *kepala desa* and splitting open a second bag for everyone else. The floor creaked and shuddered under the stampede to grab a share, then everyone sat down to the task of rolling. Premus launched forth with his introduction. Here was a showman. We'd only been with him a day but there were oohs and aahs from the crowd, peals of laughter from the boys and epiglottal cackles from the old warriors. The immediate circle of men, the leaders, listened gravely, staring solemnly at us, puffing smoke. I felt unaccountably claustrophobic and welcomed the Indonesian words that meant Premus was telling our audience about the camera. I grabbed it and went through the familiar routine while Bruce asked if we could look round the village.

Asmat villages were traditionally built on a bend in the river, the better for spotting canoe-borne raiding parties on the final approach. Spread eagled along the muddy riverbank and back seventy yards towards the forest, Fos was no exception. A single stilted boardwalk passed by each hut and the *jeu* without approaching any doors. Palm trunks laid flat over the mud and makeshift ladders provided access. The huts were small and squint. None looked as though they could keep out heavy rain. Women peered out at us as we passed but none returned a smile. It was all rather depressing.

Back in the *jeu* the conversation turned almost immediately to politics. What did we think of Indonesia? What did we think of Irian Jaya? Did we know that Indonesia was stripping bare their land and giving nothing in return? Did we know that prices here were three times those just over the border in Papua New Guinea? Everyone gave us an example of how prices differed, from T-shirts to outboard motors, until the *kepala desa* bawled at everyone of no consequence to get out. As forty boys leapt simultaneously to their feet and legged it to the various doors, the floor and roof shook, spewing dust. There was silence as he glared at a handful who had dared to stay, but they held their ground, eyes down. Through Bruce, I asked what Indonesia was taking from their land and sparked off a diatribe against the mine at Freeport and the American and Javanese interests behind it. What about trees? All gone, they said. The man on my immediate right gave the trees in question a name, a word we didn't understand but whose meaning we could guess. I looked at Premus, who mimed picking up something very heavy.

'Ironwood,' said Bruce.

Did they themselves work for the Indonesians felling the trees? The men looked uneasy. Then one spoke into the floor, a rapid, angry burst, and stalked out of the door in three strides. I looked enquiringly at Bruce.

'I don't know,' he said.

'Ask them about the *sago*,' I suggested.

He didn't need to: the man on my right picked up the word and grabbed my arm. '*Sago, tidak*! No!' he barked.

We didn't want to push the subject. Once again, we delved into our precious mountain food bags. Later I lay awake for a while and wondered about the people of Fos. Would these men also be attributing their woes to other forces working against them, forces I could only pretend to understand? The spirits of the dead could no longer be placated in the traditional manner after all, and would be making mischief in the community, the hunting grounds and the *sago* stands. When an Asmatter dies it is never believed to be through natural causes. If a man dies in his sleep, it is because his soul, wandering in the strange places of dreamtime, has been prevented by a foe from returning. If he dies while awake an enemy's magic has snatched his soul from his body. There wasn't much recourse against these dark forces, other than to use as a pillow the skull of an ancestor whose spirit would guide their own safely back. In the meantime, the lost soul, after a brief spell in the body of a hornbill, would return to roam the village in torment, haunting the people and their labours. To bring him back into the fold he had to be given a new body, carved for him out of wood, just as the first ever Asmat people had been carved into life by *Fumeripitsj*, the Windman. Then, the soul of the dead man would join the other spirits stored in the *jeu*, taking part in the decision-making and rituals of the living. Eventually the men of the village would have too many spirits on their hands. Some would have to be persuaded to leave. The head wood-carver would go into the forest to find a tree with the correct size of buttress root and, amid mock attacks by the women and children, symbolising the torment of the village at having to oust so many ancestors, it would be carried back to the *jeu*. Over the next few weeks, with stone axe and sea shell, the master carver would transform the tree into a twelve foot *bisj*, or ancestor pole, of interlocking figures representing each of the recently deceased; the most venerated warrior at the top, sporting an enormous phallus; the least venerated at the bottom, with a tiny canoe. The more skilfully carved the *bisj*, the more co-operative and honoured the spirits. When it was complete there would be a headhunting raid, then a feast of cassowary, pig, and *sago* grubs, all demonstrating to the spirits how successful and self-sufficient the village was and that their assistance was no longer required. Then the dead were encouraged to float away in the little canoe to the Asmat *Valhalla*. In some villages there was no canoe at the base and the poles were broken up and left to rot among the *sago* stands to ensure a good harvest.

The authorities had banned headhunting, forbidden all ceremonies and feasts, burned all effigies, and destroyed the *jeus*. Since the mid-eighties, largely due to the efforts of the Catholic mission, the law against longhouses had relaxed, and the art and feasts of the Asmat were making a comeback. But how many spirits were rampaging through Fos, furious at the impotence of its warriors and that their own deaths had gone unavenged?

5 YOU WILL BE CHOPPED AND BAKED!

The new millennium was just two days away. We wanted to be somewhere evocative, somewhere that looked as far removed from the twenty-first century as possible. As we had lunch in another deserted riverside hut, I asked Premus about the next village we planned to stop at. He was incising his son's forehead with a razor blade: Agus had complained of a headache and now half a dozen beads of blood flecked the skin above his eyebrows. He still had a headache but, then again, cures are rarely instantaneous.

'Not traditional. Jinak has no *jeu*. There is a shop,' he answered. 'There are no more traditional villages up this river.'

An hour later Bruce stopped paddling suddenly. 'Premus, is there a *camat* at Jinak?'

'Yes, I know him.'

A *camat* was a locally appointed headman or official answerable to the Indonesian authorities, in this case in either Agats or Senggo. Not likely to pose a problem but a small-time official nonetheless, he would be a man who would enjoy flexing his muscles at the slightest excuse. Close to the right-hand bank we cruised past a big expanse of swamp grass, brushing the tips of the overhanging stems with our paddles. A late thermal, whipping them into a violent rustle, bore down on us like an invisible tornado, but lost its growl when it ran out of grass, passing on to the water as a breath. The air was cool, the light poised for sunset. At the far side of the bend in front, tree trunks highlighted in bronze by the filtered sun appeared like a stockade wall before they were cast back into shadow. As the sky behind us turned yellow then orange, the blue darkened to cobalt, with a pink blob, the first in a line of untidy clouds stretching in from the east. It was a great excuse for me to stow my oar and get out the camera.

'How did that look?' Bruce asked, as I put it away.

'How does the front cover of *National Geographic* sound?'

Jinak was everything we did not want it to be. In the faint light still remaining a row of tin roofs and painted house fronts adorned the riverbank. We pulled in between two longboats equipped with outboard motors. Further along I could see the white hull of a fibreglass speedboat.

'Look above that white hut.' Bruce tapped my shoulder and pointed.

A television aerial, clearly silhouetted against a red cloud, was attached to a long pole, lashed in turn to the top of a palm tree. I couldn't believe that, after just four days, we had run out of interesting Asmat settlements. Neither of us had expected to find villages humming to the jungle beat of pagan rituals and brimming with skulls and fantastic carvings - we had done too much reading to be that naïve - but the most recent material in the tiny amount available dealing with this area basically hadn't mentioned it at all.

The *camat* was holding court on his veranda. His house, reached by walkways over the mud, was the white one with the television aerial. As we turned off the main walkway and along his 'garden path', a low-wattage bulb in the room behind the open door flickered into life and I heard the faint hum of a far off generator. He was affable, welcoming us boisterously and ordering two of his companions to vacate their chairs. He asked to see our travel permits and then invited us to stay. He also owned the next-door hut, which was empty. There we put up the mosquito net and spread out our mats. Afterwards we gorged on rice and catfish at the *camat's* table, served by his striking looking wife. He talked about money, and informed us of what he expected to be paid for our board and lodging. Until now we had given, as was customary, a generous contribution to the longhouses in which we had stayed but the *camat* wanted ten times that again. We decided to leave in the morning.

But in the morning our plans to celebrate the new millennium in a more photogenic place had to be abandoned. Agus was ill with what appeared to be sunstroke.

Just after dark someone lit the millennium fire, and it started to rain. Down it came, heavier and heavier, all evening. No one moved from their huts and the millennium fire went out. Shortly before midnight, determined to see it in, we were in the midst of an impressive tropical downpour. Shouting to make ourselves heard above the noise of water hammering on the tin roof, we shared a bag of dried fruit and a miniature bottle of brandy. Every few seconds lightning shattered the darkness. We toasted the big moment outside with mugs of tea. For the next hour the *camat* addressed his subjects over a tannoy system we hadn't noticed before.

The next day, when we stopped for lunch in a deserted riverside shelter, I filmed Bruce asking Premus about cannibalism. Between us a pot of stew bubbled on the fire.

'Further upriver, Premus, do they still eat people?'

'Yes, but here, not for twenty years,' the old man said matter-of-factly.

'And further upriver, are there still tribes who are at war?' Bruce asked.

'Yes, but here, not now. The village of Butukatnow, it's not OK to enter.'

'Still? Now?'

'Yes, still. If you go there you will be finished! *Bom! Pop!*' To an accompaniment of suitable noises Premus's hand shot out to stab an invisible victim then traced a cutting motion on either side of his neck. 'Cutting here and here.' He grimaced and rolled his eyes. 'They will chop you and bake you.'

Bruce laughed.

'Bake us?'

'Yes, bake you. Baking, dancing, eating meat and *sago*… Feasting.'

I wondered if Premus wasn't exaggerating but he was deadly serious. I even detected in him a glimmer of pride that his countrymen were still carrying on in such a fashion.

'Did you get all that?' Bruce asked me, when I had put the camera down.

'Pretty much.'

'Do you think it was true?'

'One of those books you found said that there had been isolated incidences of head hunting reported even in the late eighties. There aren't many police around here so I think it's safe to assume that many raids aren't reported.'

We continued to mull over what might lie ahead, like two little boys discussing Christmas presents; our excitement began to over-ride rational thought. After the meal, I wondered if I wanted to have a serious brush with death. I had had more than my fair share of close shaves already and so far had always escaped unscathed, at least physically. But if what Premus had told us was true, my next 'hit' might involve a scenario more in tune with Captain Cook's logbook than with the twenty-first century. That had been my dream when I had first got into expeditions after all – the conviction that such situations were a thing of the past had been partly responsible for my decision to try to settle down. I did not want to die on this island, or even be wounded, but to escape a volley of arrows fired by men intent on eating my brain would be brilliant.

Watching an ant scurrying about near my toes I suddenly realised I was standing on sand, not mud: we must be nearing the edge of the Asmat land for there is no stone found naturally there. The people there had used seashells to carve their ancestor poles, and nails taken from shipwreck driftwood. For stone axes they had had to travel far upstream to trade with the tribes living in the foothills - sometimes they had taken heads for barter, but whatever the cargo, it must have been a dangerous journey through enemy territory with every likelihood that the heads eventually traded for the prized stone might be their own. If you were without an axe, how did you go about getting a head to trade? A spear or arrow would kill a man but decapitation would have had to be carried out with a thighbone dagger or a fragment of shell.

As we drew closer to the confluence of the Siretsj, Eilanden and Wildeman rivers a day later the current was getting discernibly stronger. It was hot, the sun beating down on us. With socks on hands, sleeves and collar done up, and a plastic sack over my legs I was as covered up as I could be, but as we wound our way between the serpentine banks the sun consistently found new chinks in the armour.

We stopped at the village of Wooi for a short break. There was a small shelter of grass roof and four uprights with a bench along one side, just like a bus stop. A man in shorts and an imitation sola-topi perched in its shade. We joined him. He looked very old, with rheumy eyes and a body like a birch twig, but he was fine featured. But for the darkness of his skin and lack of moustache he could almost have been a Bengali, but perhaps it was the splendid hat on his head and the lack of a good one on mine that placed him in a Kipling yarn. When he looked down at his hands to roll the tobacco I had offered him, I saw his nose in profile, the blazing river sparkling through the enormous hole in his septum. At some point he must have worn a mighty ornament through it. I tried to ask if he was originally from this village but he looked at me uncomprehendingly. No one else among the men who had wandered over from other shade appeared to recognise my Indonesian either. A helpless torpor hung over the scene, as if we were all in the middle of a desert contemplating an empty water-bottle. After a cigarette I staggered off in search of Premus and Agus. They were next door, in an Indonesian style hut with an Indonesian man, being filled up with *sago*. I hovered hopefully but none was offered.

'Let's get going,' I croaked at Bruce. It was just after noon, the hottest part of the day. There was no real reason to push on but I knew Bruce wasn't going to fight it: this place was death. I led the way back to the canoe and slumped into it.

On the map, the river junction where the Eilanden both meets the Wildeman and becomes the Siretsj is like the hub of a three-spoked wheel. The spokes are of equal thickness, evenly spaced, and even lie straight, but on the river it just looks like a lot of water to cross. We needn't have crossed any of it because we were already on the left bank and turning left, and at first we didn't, but after four hundred yards Premus headed us out across the Eilanden and into the current. The canoe's bow pointed straight across the river, but I could see the far bank sweeping past it from right to left. It didn't look as though we would make it before we were carried past the last tree and out into the hub again. Without a word, we all dug in. The canoe leapt forward at each stroke, lifting itself up in the water, then settling down again as the blades flicked out of the current and back along the side. Premus nosed us upstream again with twenty yards to spare and it was clear why we had crossed. Upstream, the first bend was a right-hander and in this current we would only make headway on the inside of the corner. During the afternoon we criss-crossed the river, cutting every corner, our speed against the dense foliage reduced to the pace of a military slow march.

The next village, Karabis, was much livelier. Two parallel rows of traditional huts lined a broad strip of grass, the first expanse of solid ground I had seen since Timika and the Sheraton Hotel. More than fifty villagers fought for space on the riverbank as we docked, snatching everything, including the sandals I was trying to put on, and carrying it all to the chief's hut. There was no longhouse but, as if to make up for that, the *kepala desa* lived in a natty tin-roofed affair, on stilts that termites had almost destroyed – as they had those of the house next door, which had collapsed at an angle. Having dropped our bags within, most people came out courteously to wait for us to enter, then piled in noisily behind us. We found ourselves pinned to the right hand wall by the crush of bodies. It was incredibly hot, as you might expect under a tin roof on the equator.

Later, when the heat inside the hut had forced most people to leave, I prepared to film Bruce quizzing the *kepala desa* about the tribes living in the forest to the north, away from the main rivers. From what little information we had gleaned already we knew that our river would soon cross the northern boundary of the Asmat territory. Thereafter we would be canoeing north-east along the border between the Citak tribe to the west and Korowai tribe to the east until the strengthening current forced us to abandon the canoe and head into the jungle on foot. We had not, however, expected the current this far south to be so swift already and it was clear that the waterborne phase of the journey would end much sooner than we had planned. Cutting a path along the bank of the river was the obvious way forward but while that might be the easiest route navigationally there was a quicker way: a straight line drawn across the map to our mountain ninety miles away went through the middle of the Korowai territory.

I knew nothing about the Citak except that they were considered a sub-group of the Asmat and had also been notorious headhunters. All I knew about the Korowai was that they were thought to number some three thousand people split into tightly knit clans, that they lived in tree houses and that, to the Catholic and Protestant Churches, they had been among the most stubborn people in the whole of New Guinea. A guidebook overview of Irian Jaya's 250-odd tribes mentioned that a Dutch missionary called Gerrit van Enk had spent almost ten years in the south of the Korowai region, forbidden access to most clans on pain of death by multiple arrows; by 1990 he had failed to make a single convert. Undaunted, he had recalled that his own countrymen had taken a hundred years to embrace Christianity. Cannibalism was still frequently reported from the Korowai area.

Were these the people who might want to eat us? Premus had not been specific on tribal names and it seemed important that we arm ourselves with a little more local knowledge before we blundered into the forest with so much equipment on our backs that running was all but impossible. Clearly we should try to find van Enk, but we had no idea how to go about this other than by making a lengthy detour to ask in Senggo, where there was a police and military presence. In any case, if he had been forbidden access to the northern clans it was unlikely that he would be able to offer us more in the way of help than a lesson in Korowai etiquette. He might even see our presence as a threat to his years of hard, determined work. I didn't suppose that the aims of a mountaineer would seem important to a man who had dedicated his life to saving souls in a place he called 'the hell of the south'.

Bruce had taken these considerations a step further. 'He would probably hate us. In any case, I want us to do this on our own. Not knowing what's round the corner is half the fun.'

I agreed – I'd always thought that too much planning robbed an expedition of its soul. Risk should be assessed, not automatically avoided.

When I was happy with the camera focus and sound settings I gestured to Bruce to start the interview.

'*Bapak, orang hutan di atas sungai, mereka makan orang?* Sir, the forest people upriver, they eat people?'

Good boy, I thought.

'*Ya*. Yes,' our host responded matter-of-factly. '*Orang* Korowai. The Korowai people.'

'Still, now?'

'Yes.'

'The Korowai people?'

'Yes, the Korowai.'

I had grown used to Bruce's style of questioning. He laboured each point to encourage an unprompted response. Monosyllabic answers were not going to help us.

'Which people do they eat?' Bruce continued.

'Everyone.'

'Everyone?' Bruce's tone rose an octave.

'Everyone. They eat everyone'

'Which people? Asmat, Citak, police, Westerners?'

The *kepala desa* nodded vigorously. 'Asmat, Citak, *polis, bulay, anak-anak, Ingriss …semua!* Westerners, children, British… everyone! His eyes shone. Premus cast me an I-told-you-so look.

But I wasn't convinced. The routine cooking and consumption of anyone coming within their range would have earned the Korowai a notoriety that would have been widely publicised.

Bruce pressed on. 'Do the Korowai come here?'

'No. Korowai people only in the forest.'

'Have you been into the Korowai forest?'

'No, no, too dangerous. You cannot enter.'

'You can't enter?'

Suddenly the *kepala desa* was off. He tucked his hands into his sides, flapped his elbows as if mimicking a giant bird and began a high-pitched whooping call. '*Whoo, whoo, whoo, whoo...*' Then he broke off and mimed firing an arrow.

I was transported to the scene he was describing - being surrounded by that sound, with glimpses of shadowy figures flitting between the trees... the terror of being hunted. It was either that or in the forest ahead we were about to encounter gigantic chickens. He became still again.

'They have bows and arrows and they do not want you to enter,' he said.

'*Ah, tau...tau.* I understand.' Bruce nodded.

'*Whoo, whoo, whoo, whoo!* They wait in the tops of the trees and attack you with their arrows. *Whoo, whoo, whoo, whoo* - or they creep up on you and surround you from here and here - like this!' The *kepala desa* spread his arms wide, then scooped imaginary victims to his chest.

There was a knot in my stomach now: the hopelessness of that situation - being hunted and corralled like an animal, with no chance of negotiation, unable to escape, unable to reason with one's captors.

Now the *kepala desa* and Premus were both talking at once, well-known riverbank anecdotes, maybe, spilling out in rapid fire. I couldn't keep up, and tried only to capture on film the animated expressions on their faces. Bruce looked as if he was struggling too.

'*Peta, peta!* Map, map!' Premus looked at me imploringly and I threw our air-survey chart into the circle. In Asmat, he rattled off an explanation to the *kepala desa* as Bruce looked up the longitude and latitude of our current position, already saved in the GPS, and marked the location of Karabis against the meandering blue line of the Eilanden river.

I continued filming as the three hunched over the map. The

kepala desa had probably never seen one before and looked more than a little confused as Bruce pointed out first Karabis, then Wooi. The two crosses were less than three centimetres apart yet he knew this distance only as a four-hour canoe journey. So much paddling reduced to the length of a thumbnail was hard to assimilate and it was only when Agats was pointed out that his face showed the first signs of enlightenment. Bruce's questioning began again: where, how many, when, who? He left the two men to decide where new crosses should be drawn. Premus was getting the hang of the map: he had paddled a length of it now and knew its scale only too well. Now he studied the relief closely and landed a leathery finger not far to the north-east of our current position. Bruce threw me a conspiratorial glance across the circle. The next part of our journey was becoming more intriguing by the minute.

We went outside and rolled cigarettes on the riverbank. Another spectacular sunset was kicking-off. Pink-edged towers of cumulo-nimbus hung in the sky, their reflections illuminating passing swirls in the surface of the water.

'It would probably be easier to follow the river, but I've got to know what's in the Korowai area.' Bruce said eventually, voicing my own thoughts. There was no question about it: we had always been going to touch on the Korowai region anyway, and we had only planned to follow the river all the way because we had thought that the most interesting peoples would live along its banks. In the Asmat region nobody lived in the forest and every village was on a river. But it appeared that the Korowai were perhaps not water people. They had been able to resist the advance of the outside world for so long because there was no easy way to get to them.

'I agree,' I said. 'We'll just take the canoe as far as possible then continue on foot. I like the idea of hiding it somewhere as a possible escape route, but we're going to need porters so I suppose it will probably be at a village.'

'That's if we can find porters. You heard those two - neither of them want to go anywhere near the Korowai.'

'I think Premus might. He loves all this.'

'Maybe. I'd love it if he did come the whole way. We'd be hard pushed to find a better travelling companion and he's certainly fit enough. Do you think we're mad to leave the river?'

'No, not at all. It's what we both hoped for, isn't it?'

'Too right!' He thought for a second or two. 'If one of us ends up in the pot, the other must film it. It'll be like the *Blair Witch Project*.'

It rained heavily throughout the night, the tin roof vibrating under the ceaseless onslaught like a kettledrum being sandblasted. An evil-looking spider the size of my hand stalked prey on the wall above my head.

In the morning, with the rain still battering the tin roof above our heads it was almost ten o'clock before we could we coax our none-too-enthusiastic crew through the door to bale out *Wandy*. It was an inauspicious start to what promised to be our most difficult day yet.

The village of Binam was our next port of call and it had a police checkpoint. When we were half-way there we stopped for a strategy chat with Premus. He knew now that we planned to climb Mandala, then cross the island, but we had to impress upon him what not to reveal to the police. We told him now that we intended to travel into areas that Binam's *camat* and *polis* would not allow. Our immediate aim was to continue along the Eilanden river and ignore the only river we thought we would be allowed to enter, the Brazza. The authorities would be Indonesian, not Irianese, and they would know what tourists could and couldn't do and that the upper reaches of the Eilanden river were out of bounds. We were still considering asking Premus to stay with us for the rest of the expedition, and put out a few feelers.

The old man was spellbound by the idea. 'My last great adventure,' he said softly.

I had come to admire Premus. He was easy and uncomplicated, with an outwardly boyish exuberance that failed to disguise the tough old buzzard within.

'But Agus is not strong enough,' he said. Looking unimpressed with the prospect Agus put up no fight. He had looked unimpressed since day one, and neither Bruce nor I wanted him with us for that reason. In any case, every plan was largely academic until we had reached Binam.

It did not look like an Asmat village. A tin-roofed shop front along the bank hid another broad grassy 'street' flanked by painted huts of corrugated roof and milled wood. 'God, I hope they don't have a radio transmitter.' Bruce pointed out another television aerial lashed to a bamboo pole that protruded from the fronds of a coconut palm. The small crowd of villagers knew exactly what to do with Westerners and led us straight to the *camat*.

Bapak Hanuman, the *camat*, had come up from Merauke, on the coast, to stand in while the regular incumbent was away. He was bored, and pleased at the diversion we provided. A tub of biscuits was placed on the table before us. Careful not to mention river names, Bruce told him falsely that we desired to trek to Wamena. In reverse, this had been done before, and starting from the south, while possibly a first, might not raise any eyebrows. He also asked casually about the Korowai tribe. If we could get his permission to turn right at the next confluence of rivers then so much the better - but we were the *camat's* first tourists and he was unforthcoming: he was not fully versed on the rules or the area.

At that point a neighbour joined us. Supratman, in his early thirties, with long hair, moustache, singlet and jeans, knew all about the Korowai. With little prompting, he told us about the area we wished to enter. 'Oh, yes, the people there are completely untouched by the outside.' He related how he had once watched two men laboriously fell a tree with stone axes, and how unimpressed they had been when he, with a *parang*, had lopped a foot from the stump in less than a third of the time.

The policeman arrived and asked for our papers. He was officially friendly. Suddenly everybody was talking too quickly for me. I could almost see the alarm bells ringing in Bruce's head as he tried to keep up.

'No, you cannot travel up the Eilanden,' the law announced in a manner that did not invite argument.

'But we only want to go up the Brazza!' Bruce was back-paddling.

'But the traditional tribes live up the Eilanden,' Supratman insisted. 'Up the Brazza they are only a little bit traditional.'

'Traditional people good for camera,' Premus added unhelpfully.

I made a face at him.

'Not possible!' The policeman was showing signs of annoyance. 'The Brazza, maybe. I will keep these,' he held up our passports and travel permits,' and radio Senggo in the morning.'

After he had gone, Bruce said, 'I've got a bad feeling about this.' I asked him to fill me in with all I had missed.

'We can't leave here by canoe. The current gets too strong just above the confluence and this is the last place we can hire a longboat. We wouldn't reach a village and porters in the canoe on either river. If we leave in *Wandy* they'll become suspicious.'

'And we can't slip away on foot because we'll need porters.'

'Yup. I don't want to go in a speedboat but it looks like the only way out of here.' This expedition, of course, was supposed to use traditional means of transport only.

'If it's the only way of getting through this it's a justifiable compromise. We won't have betrayed the principles of the expedition. It'll only be a couple of hours.'

'It's not just that. The only speedboat here at the moment belongs to the *camat*. It'll be his driver.'

'Oh.' I pondered this for a while. 'What if we canoe back down to Karabis, hire porters there, then chop a path to the north-east, past this place?'

'Even if we did get porters, and I bet there'd be problems, it would take days to get past here. Sod's Law - we'd meet someone in the forest and word would spread. I want to get away from that policeman as quickly as possible. I don't trust him. Supratman might be an ally – I'll go and talk to him. Can you make sure Premus doesn't talk to the *camat*? He might drop us in it if we're not careful.'

The evening continued like this, plan and counter-plan, none going anywhere. Bruce was wary of revealing all to Supratman - he was the policeman's neighbour and friend - but without all the facts he remained noncommittal. I longed to film the proceedings but the two boxes had to remain hidden: we were just tourists now.

Next day the sun was already overhead when the policeman returned. Yes, we could go up the Brazza river, was all he said. We were elated. At least we could continue upstream without arousing suspicion.

'Now we've just got to bribe the driver,' Bruce said. 'I'm going to tell Supratman everything and try to hire him as a guide. How much can we afford?'

'Whatever it takes. We'll have to lose Premus.' The *camat* wanted £250 for the hire of his boat and driver – exorbitant, but this was not the time for quibbling. I counted it out in our biggest notes.

Supratman was a willing accomplice, tickled at the idea of outwitting the police and happy with the ten pounds per day plus return-leg expenses he had agreed with Bruce.

'How much?' I exploded.

'We need him! He knows the driver, says there won't be a problem. Oh, and he's bringing a friend.'

The gang of small boys who helped me carry the bags to the riverbank feigned indignation at the 500 *rupiah* (5p) with which I rewarded each of them. Heinrich Harrer never had it this bad, I thought, shooing them away. When Bruce, Supratman and Premus turned up, I was adding to our pile another sack of rice. We took Premus aside and sat on a log next to three men who were hacking a longboat out of a truly gigantic tree trunk. Before we could tell him we had decided we must leave him behind, he said that although he would love to come with us he had to take Agus home. Disappointment was written all over his face. We were relieved that the decision had come from him, but were still sad to lose him. Tears came into his eyes when we gave him our hardback copy of Heinrich Harrer's *I came from the Stone*

Age. He had looked at it often, fingering the photographic plates reverently and muttering with fresh pleasure at each viewing.

On the point of clambering aboard the longboat, I glanced wistfully at the canoe swinging lazily in the current, and suddenly realised we had forgotten about it. The obvious recipient was Premus but I had not thought to include it in his redundancy package. We gave it to him anyway, and his uncharacteristic look of despondency vanished.

The longboat's noisy outboard motor made light work of the steadily increasing current and in an hour we had covered what might have taken a day in the canoe. It was Binam's only motorboat, or at least the only one moored there during our stay, so no one would give chase, and the atmosphere lightened.

A neat spit of sand guides the waters of the Brazza river into that of the larger Eilanden. We motored on to it like a landing craft disgorging troops. On the principle of need-to-know, the driver's time had come. Supratman did the talking. I watched the unsuspecting face for an adverse reaction, but need not have worried. We motored ahead, leaving the silted water of the Brazza undisturbed and the Asmat region behind.

Now the current picked up, the surface of the water torn by innumerable trees and branches. Our newest collaborator picked a passage through these at half-speed, slowing almost to a halt through particularly tangled or shallow stretches. Squeezed into the narrow bow alongside Bruce and me, Supratman operated a long pole as a plumb line, calling back to the helmsman at each submerged hazard. A tree, high and dry on a gravel shoal, illustrated the river's power in the rainy season. Still intact, it was vast - fully two hundred feet long with giant buttresses at its base, like an abandoned intergalactic rocket with its nose cone embedded in a bush. The black mud of the banks downstream had now given way to red earth and bleached stones. A four-metre cliff of it with a gaggle of unkempt onlookers on top, confronted us as we pulled in at Mabul. There was one more village further on, apparently, but Mabul was as far upstream as the driver would risk taking us. Either that or he couldn't wait another minute for his tip - the river ahead looked no worse than it had been thus far. Now he stood at the edge of the water, holding the boat and watching as we unloaded the gear.

'*Dua juta stenga!*' he said with relish. He wanted the equivalent of £250.

Bruce looked at me: by mutual consent I had become the paymaster general. 'Like hell!' I responded succinctly.

'I do not want to piss him off,' said Bruce.

'If he goes back and tells all he'll be dropping Supratman, who's his friend, right in it and perhaps even himself. We can get it for much less.'

Bruce translated my concerns to the claimant: we would if we could but we couldn't - such an outlay would leave us unable to return to our families, destitute, at the mercy of the *polis*. The man accepted the equivalent to eighty pounds - still a fortune - and climbed back into his boat, hopefully still thinking we were good people and did not deserve the trouble he could unleash upon us.

'Where's the rice?' I asked, scanning the pile of kit now on the riverbank for the fresh bag.

'Premus had a bag of rice when we left,' Supratman said brightly.

I was somewhat annoyed to hear this – we would need to buy more food if the dried rations were going to last until the mountains for which we'd brought them. Bruce laughed and I had to also. I didn't think Premus had stolen the rice, simply that there had been a mix-up.

6 THE BECKONING JUNGLE

Mabul had been built by the Indonesian authorities: sixteen stilted houses lined a grassy strip, traditionally roofed but walled with sawn planks. It was part of an incentive scheme, we were told, to entice people out of the forest and into the 'fold'. It looked like a camp. The people around us were Korowai who had been enticed and didn't look too happy about it. They had the air of refugees trapped in a no man's land between the forest and the modernisation brought by the river in front. Shorts, skirts and T-shirts, all dirty and torn, hung on their chunky frames and seemed to illustrate how ill-fitted they were for change. Some of the men smiled in welcome and helped us with our bags, but most hung back in silent apprehension. In halting Indonesian, we were invited to stay in the house nearest the river, and the village followed us in, settling on the floor in a packed crescent before us while we rummaged around for an offering of tobacco. It was the icebreaker. We were clearly not here to assess or interfere, and everyone relaxed.

The people of Mabul differed from Asmatters in both stature and appearance. The men seemed shorter than those we had grown used to, averaging perhaps five foot one, their skin a shade lighter. Their faces were more compact and round, their noses flatter. They looked healthy but my eyes were drawn to a teenage boy whose left knee had disappeared within a grotesque black and yellow swelling running from mid-thigh to his ankle. It didn't appear to hurt but without medical attention whatever was going on inside it would surely kill him. The nearest doctor was in Senggo. I suggested he should go there but his response was dismissive.

This was our first opportunity to talk casually with Supratman and Kasim, his friend. Kasim was one of the Marind-Anim people from the south-eastern corner of the province, near Merauke. The name rang a bell. I told him that the first people to cross the island had hired their porters from his people because they were strong. To our astonishment, he told us that his grandfather had been on a journey across Irian Jaya before the Dutch had gone away. It had to have been the same expedition. What a remarkable coincidence, I thought, and how unlikely that Kasim would want anything more to do with us. Bruce was thinking likewise. 'Let's hope the old boy wasn't much of a storyteller.' He nudged me in the ribs. 'That was the stalked-by-death expedition.'

Supratman was excited by the prospect of crossing the island, but Kasim had gone very quiet. We negotiated by candlelight for five porters. Supratman had quickly grasped our requirements and budget, but had a hard time against some persistent bargainers. A daily rate of R30,000 (£3) plus R5,000 for food was agreed and, in addition, for they seemed keen to go all the way to the mountain with us, R15,000 a day for their return journey to Mabul. The only major concession we made was to agree to cross the Eilanden once more after a day's walk. We could return to the eastern side a day later, we were told. The reason for the detour was unclear but the men before us were adamant that it was necessary.

As the discussion ended I wondered if they had understood our intentions. Our map had generated not a flicker of understanding and their command of Indonesian was little better than mine. Despite their assurances we had not the slightest idea for how long they would be with us. But we had no alternative. We might not come across many more villages at which to hire others along our route - there were none marked on any map.

Bruce was pleased with Supratman. He was a good find, he reckoned. We had not aimed to take an Indonesian with us because of the effect their presence might have on our relationship with the Irianese, but Supratman looked as far removed from a figure of authority as we could have hoped for, the very antithesis of the gun-toting Rambos we might have been lumbered with. While he spoke neither English nor Korowai, it was already clear that he would reduce the number of misunderstandings between our porters and us. To his delight we nicknamed him Superman.

As the bags were carried out into the damp morning air Kasim announced he would not be accompanying us. Superman was dismissive: 'He is weak.'

The loads were split and split again until they were of equal weight. The porters lifted each tentatively, then argued over which was whose. I wrote their names on their respective loads in black marker-pen. Yirus, the strongest-looking, was clearly the unelected leader and spokesman, despite his relative youth. He appeared to speak more Indonesian than the others and his bearing was confident. He had been at the forefront of the previous day's negotiations. Stocky and muscular, he had the squashed, upturned nose of a pug, and intelligent eyes that seemed reluctant to meet mine. Bangol, Laville and Yalil were older, perhaps in their thirties, and of the silent type. I liked the look of Laville. Squatting quietly beside his bag, he wore an expression of unassailable calm. He, too, was reluctant to look me in the eye. Bangol had an emaciated leg, which I pointed out to Superman.

'Don't worry,' he assured me, 'they are very tough.' Labalaba was a boy - I pointed this out too. '*Kohat*! Strong,' said Superman reproachfully.

'*Tidak masala* No problem,' said Labalaba, hefting his load easily. He was sixteen or seventeen, and lightly built, with more enthusiasm and life in his big round eyes than the rest put together.

'Labalaba means 'spider' in Indonesian. Draw one on his load,' Bruce said, and at last everyone was laughing.

I stopped laughing when I hoisted my own load on to my shoulders. At over forty kilos our rucksacks weighed more than twice what the porters were carrying. Mine felt like a house - but it also felt fantastic to be away, on foot and into we knew not what. A small crowd saw us off from the front of the hut we had stayed in. They seemed unmoved, as if their menfolk were going out for a day to fetch some bananas. I was so busy doing up the straps hanging from my rucksack that I didn't notice anything strange or ominous in that at the time.

At the far end of the grass strip the porters sprang neatly on to a log that bridged a small swamp and disappeared into the trees. I waited for Bruce to catch up. When he did I indicated the log. 'After you.'

'No, no, I insist.'

I stepped on to the log. My boot slid straight off and into the water. 'Uh-oh…'

Little more than an hour later, I called for a quick break. My shoulders felt permanently deformed.

'Yeah, they are a bit heavy, aren't they?' For the first time I noticed how annoying Bruce's giggle was.

'I've got to lose some of it,' I said. On clear ground I could have coped with the weight but this was not clear ground. A tangled mess of roots and logs sat on top of semi-solid humus and over watery swamp. The lie of the land was flat but I had to fight to keep my balance as my feet shot off in unexpected directions on the slimy wood or sank out of sight in glue-like mud. My ligaments and tendons were complaining already. 'It's only just occurred to me that we're a porter short anyway. We never replaced Kasim.'

'Do you want to go back and get another?'

'Definitely not. I just want to lose the rope, grappling-hook and black box. Superman's carrying sod all, and, frankly, so are the porters.'

'I want to lose my rope too. We can take it in turns with the orange box.'

Superman took over the black box graciously and the four older porters each accepted some more, and we set off again.

It was a beautiful forest of tall, straight trees that allowed more light through to the ground than I had expected, but there wasn't a corresponding explosion of impenetrable growth between the trunks. We agreed that, as jungles went, this was by no means the most difficult we had come across. The porters chattered away noisily, hardly looking at their feet as they walked. Their splayed toes found easy grip on the logs and fallen trees. In front of me Bruce was staggering around like a drunk finding his way home across a freshly ploughed field. What did we look like to them? As we sat around eating lunch, I was glad I didn't understand their language - I'd have been threatening to dock their pay for cheek.

In mid-afternoon - thank God - we reached a small shelter built near the Eilanden. The feeling of weightlessness you experience when you finally drop a heavy load, was bliss.

'These boys don't know it yet,' I said, 'but Father Christmas is in their midst, and this is his sack.' I kicked my rucksack.

'What are you going to give away?' Bruce asked.

'Lots. The pleasure gained from trekking is inversely proportional to the weight carried, and I am carrying too much.' I was rather pleased with that statement. Soon the contents of my pack were strewn over the ground but, depressingly, I couldn't see much to give away. The spare bar of soap, two shirts, a pair of shorts and two pairs of thick socks that I could dump would make barely any difference to the load. There was nothing else I would not miss: the mosquito repellent might be a lifesaver, the bivouac bag would be vital on the mountain, the hammock would be a Godsend on the impossibly steep and overgrown foothills. The rest was camera equipment, and the satellite phone we had brought to keep in touch with our sponsors. Only one item begged closer scrutiny. I went very quiet. Superman's breathing picked up a pace.

The following morning I felt no grief at the loss of the sleeping bag, and those few pounds made all the difference. As if in confirmation, Bruce had a tough day, setting an excruciatingly slow pace through the forest. Sensing the possibility of more goodies, the porters watched him closely, like wolves trailing an old, infirm member of a caribou herd.

As agreed, we crossed the river. In Mabul I had assumed this was going to involve a canoe but the Eilanden at this point was an easy wade and no wider than before. It was only when I looked at the map in detail that I realised we had not crossed the river. The Eilanden was earning its name: it had split in two and we were on a vast island.

The ground was wet and frequently submerged. Almost every hour we were presented with a major tree bridge. Some were so high and slippery that we could not afford to refuse the help offered by either Superman or the porters. It grated with me a little to have a man walking backwards in front of me, holding both my hands and making encouraging noises, and Bruce was dismayed too, but we had no choice. We knew that to fall off would almost certainly involve a broken bone, and to wade through the mud and deep water below would take too long. We swallowed our pride.

'I feel like a damn fairy princess!' Bruce sulked.

In the early afternoon, we came to another small shelter. Inside it, a powerfully-built man was flanked by a pair of wives and two young daughters. A third child was just visible in a string bag on the younger woman's back. I failed to spot it at first: I was too engrossed in the ornaments worn by the older members of the family. The patriarch sported a boar's tusk through his septum, and fine needles of wood protruded from the end of his nose in a symmetrical porcupine-like display. A line of equally spaced circular scars tracked from each forearm to his shoulders, then down again, past the nipple, to his waist. The girls each wore several bracelets, necklaces, and earrings of wood, bone and teeth threaded along spun string. Through Yirus I asked the man about his scars. They were called *ngawalalun*, and had been self-inflicted: he had placed glowing rolls of bark on each spot then left them there until they had burnt away. I must have looked suitably impressed because Yirus felt compelled to assure me that this had been done over a period of several years. It was decorative rather than the mark of an initiation, we discovered. Everyone did it, by choice.

The family was on a trip away from their village to harvest some bananas. Like *sago* palms, these had belonged to the same family for generations. Self-seeded, perhaps, and miles from their owners' home, they still needed no fences or guards. In a society whose number is largely governed by available food, nothing is more sacred than the ownership of that food. Nobody would interfere with a tree showing signs of custody by another. Even raiding headhunters were known to have respected this.

We marched onwards until an orange, polypropylene awning, adorning a stilted hut, appeared about a mile in front of us on a bend in the river. Desperate to drop my rucksack, I found a new speed along the boggy path as it snaked around an impassable swamp. That last half-mile took a lifetime but at last just one vast tree bridge over a deep inlet lay between me and the crudely chopped clearing.

The orange hut was perched high on the steep riverbank and, beside it, a blue one. The perpetrator of the destruction that surrounded them lived with his wife and small boy in the latter. He was a bit of a dude, in a battered Homburg and shorts, his nose and ears decorated and pierced to distraction. The child became speechless at the sight of us, and remained so throughout the ordeal. The wife never came out of their hut. The sun had not far to go so we rushed to set up our hammocks among the fallen trees. Mr Homburg cut some sticks for me to suspend my basha sheet from and peered through the sewn-in mosquito net in perplexity. How did one get into the hammock? He was cautious when I showed him the slit entrance in the underside and invited him to try it, then I left him to climb in and out, shrieking with laughter. The porters, ensconced in the orange hut, ignored the commotion - they had all had a go last night. Tonight they had other things on their minds.

The following morning we were supposed to cross the river again. It was too deep and powerful to wade, but as a man living on an island, Mr Homburg had a canoe. It was time to get back into the Korowai forest and follow a compass-bearing to the mountain. The porters would have none of this. Yirus led the rebellion. Bangol, Laville and Yalil showed dissent also but I could not tell how much this was due to Yirus or their own opinions. But it didn't matter: they would certainly go with Yirus whatever. Labalaba was clearly torn. After several hours' arguing we had made no progress. They were afraid to go through that part of the forest because people who would attack them lived there. Eventually we arrived at a compromise. We would all stay where we were for another night and in the morning Bruce, Superman and I would go into the forest for a few days while they stayed with Mr Homburg. We had to see what all the fuss was about. Calm settled over the clearing. Mr Homburg produced a pile of forest produce for the days ahead, and the porters fell upon it with determination. We had been warned in books and in person that if food is made available the Irianese will eat everything at once, even making themselves sick to complete the task. We had paid little attention and weren't really aware of quite how much they were all getting through. In fact we were too busy tucking in ourselves. There was *sago*, cucumbers and a delicious inner stem from some type of large grass, baked green bananas, sweet potatoes and *matoa* berries. We lay in the sun on a stilted platform, picking at a banana-leaf platter of local delicacies like Roman aristocrats at the height of the empire.

When I woke in the morning, argument had broken out again beneath the orange roof and we discovered that Yirus and Labalaba would now accompany us. This was good news, and not just because we now had a better chance of communicating with whoever we might meet: it was also a relief not to be leaving all the food, with much of the tobacco and the presents, with all of the porters. I didn't trust them.

. First we had to cross the river in Mr Homburg's canoe. Laville and Bangol ferried us across two fast-flowing channels in four trips. As he waited at the half-way point Bruce tried to get to grips with the various Korowai clans. It was an all but impossible task.

We didn't know then that there were fifty contacted, or 'pacified', clans within the Korowai territory, thirty-seven others who were known by name but not yet located, and many more unidentified ones thought to exist. We didn't know that it was not yet understood where the northern border of the Korowai lay, or that those clans in the north remained uncontacted because they would still attack any outsider who ventured into their territories. We didn't know that there were more villages like Mabul along the Becking river further to the east. We didn't know that no one was thought to have had any contact with the Korowai until a handful of missionaries had begun work in 1978 and that when the clans had first glimpsed them they had thought the end of the world had come. We didn't know that the Korowai were not thought to have practised head-hunting but had themselves been on the menu of the neighbouring Citak tribe, which was why they feared the outside and outsiders. We didn't know that cannibalism was certainly still practised, nor that as trespassing outsiders we were about to become known as *laleo*, which means 'bad spirit' or 'demon', and were quite likely to be riddled with arrows if we entered the wrong clan territory.

We knew nothing.

In the limited time we had allowed for planning we hadn't even discovered that an anthropological linguistic study had been published in 1997 by the two missionaries who had had more contact with the Korowai than anyone else, detailing all of the above and even including a Korowai-English dictionary.

In the six weeks before our departure we'd carried out as much research as we could but it was a paltry effort considering where we were going. Now I can take some comfort from the fact that we had not set out with the explicit aim of exploring Korowai territory. Only curiosity of the unknown was now leading us to venture away from the river. We were completely unqualified to know what we were doing, other than having a look.

So, on the island, sitting close together on the grey stones, we discovered that, thus far, we had met members of the Besi and the Suka Duka clans. Mr Homburg and the family of two days ago were of the former, and our porters were of the latter, all now living outside their traditional clans. There were also, we were told, clans called the Batu and the Khanum Khatun. The Batu were contacted but not the Khanum Khatun and the porters were terrified of them. It all seemed reasonably clear at the time. However, while Suka Duka and Khanum Khatun sounded local,

Besi and Batu were recognisable Indonesian words – meaning iron and stone. Was this coincidence, or had the Indonesians gathered together different clan names into easier classifications? Superman hadn't a clue, and no one seemed to have any idea whom we might stumble across in the area we now planned to hack our way through. This was perhaps why Yirus was glaring at us as we loaded the canoe for the second leg of the crossing.

It was much later that I learned that the inhabitants of Mabul came from ten different clans. I have found no mention of Suka Duka anywhere and my confusion would be complete but for the fact that there are several known clan names ending in Khatun, and that Batu was indeed a collective name, given to those clans living along the river.

'Don't worry about him. He is just afraid.' Superman was enjoying his role as guide, though how much guiding he was doing was debatable: Bruce and I had decided where we wanted to go and what direction would take us there. It was roughly the same area that Superman had told us about visiting two years before, but he had come in from a different direction and without a map. I defied him to find it again.

Safely delivered to the far side we walked along exposed riverbed for a while, then turned in towards the 150-foot wall of vegetation. Amid the shimmer of heat rising from the pale stones I stopped to film the party disappearing into its green fastness. The chatter and screech of invertebrates was at a staggering volume, like a frenzied warning from tribal spirits to 'keep out of forbidden territory'. A surge of excitement gripped me as I stepped from the light open space into the dark, the creepers and leaves closing behind me as I pushed through. At the same moment the crunch of my boots against river stones died, replaced by the soft squelch of decomposing vegetation. Even Yirus and Labalaba fell silent as the sound of the river receded behind us.

7 THE KOROWAI

Superman, unimpeded by any serious weight on his shoulders, took the lead. Having to chop our way through should have slowed us down but somehow the going was easier, less cluttered, and drier underfoot. There was a great deal of weaving around swampy stands of *sago* palms but by midday we had covered a respectable distance on the map. I was feeling peckish and I could hear the sound of a small river in front.

'Mr Bruce! Mr Mark! *Tidak bechara*! Stop talking!' Superman was crouching, and gesticulating with his *parang* that we do likewise. Silently we crept forward to where he lay at the base of a tree and peered through the undergrowth between the river and us. I gathered from him that there were two boys on the far bank. Bruce was already filming, but I couldn't see a damn thing. A moment later I had just focused on them when they froze and looked in our direction. As Superman leapt forward and called a greeting they legged it. Only when Yirus and Labalaba called out did one of the boys re-emerge from the bushes. He stood still, but looked poised for flight. Bruce and I waited until he seemed to relax a little, then stepped on to the shingle and into the sunlight.

The boy, who was perhaps fifteen, was hesitant as we put our bags down on the shingle at the water's edge. He was about twenty-five metres from us and watched our every move. I gave him top marks for courage, but was certain he would suddenly be overwhelmed by it all and vanish. I was wrong. He came into the water and clumsily grasped Superman's outstretched hand, then they both splashed back towards the shingle. When I stepped forward with my own hand outstretched the boy backed off again. I felt like a Dalek. At Superman's insistence, I retreated and sat on my pack. Bruce was holding the camera at waist-level, keeping an eye on the screen, and filmed the drama.

Encouraged by the few words they had heard the boy speak Yirus and Labalaba advanced to explain Bruce and me in their own tongue. Visibly relieved, but still darting nervous glances towards us, the boy spoke in a rush. As far as first meetings went, this had been beyond our wildest dreams: the setting, the boy, his reactions - none of it had seemed of the modern age, let alone the new millennium. It seemed almost a shame that we had Yirus and Labalaba with us. How much more rewarding it would have been to gain the boy's trust through sign language.

The boy wore a length of rattan tied round his waist, and a piece of leaf rolled and tied round his foreskin in a manner that looked less to do with decorative effect than with keeping things from crawling up it. His hair was cropped short. His body was lithe, well developed and glowed with health. He made us, in our mud and sweat-soaked clothes, look shabby and poor.

At last he allowed Bruce and me to come close enough to clasp hands and steer the dialogue. What was his name? We wanted to know where he lived and with whom – would he take us there? No, he certainly would not! I found myself nodding - I wouldn't have taken us there either. His name was Ayare, and he assured us that his father and many more men were close by. His father would be angry if he were to take us to where they lived. We offered him a necklace of cowrie shells interspersed with a few beads, but he had set his sights on other things. To our horror both Yirus and Labalaba stood up and each took off an article of clothing: Yirus his T-shirt, Labalaba his shorts - both items I had off-loaded.

'I never saw that coming. We could do real damage here.' Bruce was as appalled as I was.

'No more gifts,' Bruce told Superman, and tried to explain why we thought this had been wrong. He was perplexed, and Yirus and Labalaba looked nonplussed. Suddenly Ayare got up and announced that he was going to fetch his father.

For a while we sat in the sun and pondered the selection of

gifts we had bought just before boarding the ship in Bali. The early-twentieth-century visitors to New Guinea had given steel knives and axe heads to the people they encountered, but neither Bruce nor I had felt that was the right thing to do. We had brought a handful of small pocket knives and a bundle of craft-knife blades but we had chosen the bulk of our presents on the advice of friends in Jakarta, and in line with our desire not to introduce anything that might change the way that people such as these lived. So, our gifts consisted mainly of cowrie-shell and plastic-bead necklaces. We hoped these would soon fall apart – as anything bought in that part of Bali usually does – rather than supersede whatever the recipients normally made for themselves. We had also brought a bag of salt, some rough tobacco and a handful of fishing hooks attached to short lengths of line. Nothing too corruptive there – tobacco grows everywhere in New Guinea and is smoked by all.

The next person to appear was an old man carrying a piglet in the crook of one arm and his hunting weaponry in the other. We suddenly noticed him standing near the same spot where Araye had vanished, watching us silently through the shadows. When he realised he had been spotted he strode across the river, giving us scarcely a second glance until he reached our side where he observed us from twenty metres away. I asked Yirus to remind me of the greeting and advanced to say hello. I didn't get far: he directed a few curt words to Yirus, ignoring me, then turned on his heel and disappeared upstream.

We waited again. Superman had visited a *matoa* tree and had dragged back a branch laden with berries. Similar in taste and texture to lychees, I found them irresistible and competed with him for the last few. This little clearing could have been a corner of the Garden of Eden, I thought, with its crystal clear river, its trees, the abundance of fruit, and the aura of discreet symbiosis. I knew it was not typical of the forest around me but enjoyed its clean simplicity nonetheless. Over the bank behind me was a different reality: insects, putrefaction, soggy boots and vicious thorny plants.

Soon Ayare returned with his father. The older man looked very young to be the father of a teenager. His name was Diyale, and he wore a narrow, black, rubber headband, fashioned from a car inner tube, but was otherwise dressed as his son was. We gave him a necklace and a fishing hook, and asked if we might see his home. He shook his head. I leant forward to touch his headband. It was the only physical sign we had seen so far that indicated contact with the outside world but the nearest car was hundreds of miles away. Where had he got it? He pointed at the river and mimed the drawing back of a bowstring. I didn't understand what he meant, but I knew it wasn't likely to have floated down the river.

We were disappointed to hear that they lived in a house on high stilts rather than in a treehouse. In 1996, a group of Korowai people living near the Becking river had appeared in the National Geographic magazine living in fantastic houses built in the very tops of trees, 150 feet from the ground. In Jakarta we had learnt that in that area they had come down from the heights in recent years because the threat of inter-clan conflict had diminished. Here, they were still living high up, though: Diyale pointed half-way up the trees behind us as an indication. Neither Bruce nor I needed to exaggerate our delight at this.

The conversation had begun to dry up when Diyale suddenly got to his feet and strode away. Half-way across the river he stopped and bent forward, hands clasped behind his back, until his face was in the shallow water. He drank for a few seconds, then vanished into the trees. We sat in silence, gazing towards the trees and undergrowth into which he had so deftly and smoothly disappeared.

Nobody was quite sure what, if anything, would happen next and the sun was setting. We set up an A-frame shelter for Superman, Labalaba and Yirus on the cooling riverbed stones, then our own hammocks in a double-decker affair between the only two suitable trees that were close by. Ayare helped us collect firewood and stayed with us for a while, illuminated by the ensuing flames as he and Yirus talked. Later, as I lay under the

A-frame writing my diary, Superman and Labalaba prowled the river, like a pair of herons looking for a fish supper. Occasionally their torch would illuminate them standing motionless in the water, waiting for a fish to enter the beam within *parang* range. Shouts of triumph and the sub-aqua 'tock' of steel hitting rock accompanied each slash at the water, competing with the evening chorus of crickets and cicadas. Later I was presented with two freshly-barbecued fish the size of whitebait, my *parang*, blade trashed, and my torch, batteries flat.

'Why, thank you, Superman!'

'*Tidak masalah*, No problem, Mr Mark. *Enak!* Delicious!'

They were indeed delicious, or at least one was - I dropped the other on my way to the hammocks and it was too small to find again.

In the morning, after two baked bananas, I waded downstream for a while. When I returned Bruce was surrounded by six naked men, among them Diyale.

Bruce was annoyed that I hadn't been there to help him film their approach. In fact, though we didn't know it, he'd captured beautifully the almost aggressive speed with which the men had come to him across the stones. They had all but crossed the river before anyone noticed. In a tight group they had marched straight past Superman, Yirus and Laba and right to his feet.

Aiming from the hip he had captured the men's reactions to the novelty of a handshake, their closed hands colliding with, then grabbing his fingertips.

When I turned up he had overcome his initial shock and was showing the men seated before him how to roll a cigarette using papers rather than the tobacco leaves they were used to. He asked if they had ever seen people like us before. The response was a unanimous 'No'. Pointing at Superman, however, they said they had seen his like once before. I fished out the beads and presented a necklace to each man. They seemed to like them but 'indifferent' wouldn't be too far wide of the mark either. Fishing hooks were more popular and the bag of salt was very nearly a hit. Once again there was no weaponry in evidence and we asked about this. As one they rose and strode across the river, and almost immediately returned, each carrying a bow and half a dozen arrows. Either they had stashed them just round the corner, so as not to alarm us perhaps, or their homes were just a few hundred yards away.

The bows and arrows were about five feet long. The bows were all a deep, reddish-brown, beautifully polished from ceaseless handling, and strung with rattan. They were also powerful, requiring some effort to draw the string back a few inches. There was a bewildering array of arrows. I picked out five main types of arrowhead and, with sign language, established the prey for which each was designed. They were all mounted on bamboo shafts without flights, and bound neatly in place with bark-fibre string. A bamboo blade, smooth and elliptical like that of an *assegai*, was for shooting pigs. A straight, smooth hardwood spike seemed to be multi-purpose, while another simple spike, this time cut with fine barbs, was for cassowary. The fourth was a delicate four-pronged affair of splayed bamboo spikes that, like the spread of lead from a shotgun, increased the chance of hitting a bird. The last, an ugly, flat-bladed thing with massive carved barbs, was for men.

I mimed squeezing juice from a plant, smearing it on an arrowhead, touching my tongue and feigning instant death, but they shook their heads. Did that mean they didn't use poison, or just that these points were not poisoned? Yirus didn't understand either and I never found out.

Sitting down again, attention switched to the camera and I showed them their images on the screen. Each man's face was a study of unruffled calm. Only one leant forward for a closer look. There was an awkward silence. I looked at Bruce for suggestions.

'Geography lesson!' He leapt to his feet and dived into one of the sacks beneath the A-frame. We all watched as he blew up the beachball-sized globe. Of course we were both aware that pointing at a plastic balloon and saying, 'That's where we come from,' was going to be confusing to men who didn't even have a horizon to look at, but his performance did raise a few laughs.

Laughter was perhaps the best we could hope for. All we wanted was to win enough trust for them to invite us to follow them through that tantalising gap in the bushes on the other side of the river. In one of their houses, not here, we would discover more about their lifestyle and customs. It didn't matter that we were not their first contact with the outside world: if they had been uncontacted we would perhaps never have got even this far. The rubber band around Diyale's head, and the old hunter's reaction yesterday had indicated that someone else might have met them and that we might have a chance of going a step further, perhaps satisfying some of their curiosity as well as ours.

But as we moved into the shade beneath the A-frame I could feel this slipping from our grasp. It was becoming apparent that we were no longer directing the flow of conversation. Yirus was no longer smiling and had begun to dominate the proceedings, talking loudly, almost aggressively, to the Korowai and all but ignoring us. We had no idea what he was telling them or how he was translating our questions but the atmosphere was becoming less friendly. Labalaba looked uncomfortable.

'I think Yirus is working against us here.' I rolled a cigarette during another of his tirades.

Bruce was fidgeting with frustration. 'I'm certain he is. We're not even getting straight answers to simple questions. I think he's protecting them for some reason, turning them against us so they won't allow us in. I wish we'd never brought him.'

As a last-ditch attempt to illustrate the innocence of our interest in their lives, we used sign language to bypass Yirus and persuaded them to demonstrate how they started a fire with the strips of rattan they wore, either wound tightly round their waists or plaited round a biceps. One went off to find the other ingredients. A dry stick of about two inches in diameter was partially split down the middle and a stone wedged between the two halves to keep them apart. This was placed on top of a pile of tinder, the open split vertical, and held there by the firelighter's feet. The rattan strip, wound at each end round a smaller stick acting as a handle, ran between wood and tinder, pulled firmly to and fro in a sawing action to create the heat. The purpose of the split was made clear when the demonstrator stopped sawing to blow gently through the gap on to the smoking grass beneath. I stood by to applaud the impending flames but they never came despite more than five attempts by three men. At best, this was evidently a tiresome chore. In the end, one asked me to light his tobacco.

Back in the shade, I sensed that the meeting was ending. I couldn't think of anything else we could try in order to change their minds. Needing something to do, I examined the damaged blade of my *parang*, watched by one man sitting apart from the rest. He ran his finger over the dents along the edge then tapped them with a stone, looking at me enquiringly. I nodded, and we laughed together at the understanding. Encouraged again, I asked in sign language if he had an axe. He stood up and joined the others. I went down to the water's edge, twenty feet away, and set about repairing my blade with a whetstone. Disappointing as it was, I thought we were bound to have other opportunities to get to know some clansmen between here and the foothills. Also I felt guilty: it would have been fine if I could classify myself as a visitor who offered only friendly exchange but I couldn't - we had a television camera with us. Like the missionaries we had hidden motives yet unlike the missionaries ours were selfish: we were not filming for any reason that might help the Korowai, only to ensure we had footage good enough to make it to television.

After a particularly long outburst from Yirus the men stood up, abruptly, and left. I watched their sleek bodies splash across the river and blend into the dappled backdrop of green and brown, light and shadow. As they crossed they shouted something back to us. We looked at Yirus.

'If we are still here this night we will be dead,' he said.

We didn't wait around to call anyone's bluff and had packed up within half an hour. Ayare appeared again during this time and sat on a stone watching us. I was pleased to see that he was no longer wearing the shorts and T-shirt. We said goodbye to him and left, following the path by which we had arrived.

Despite all our efforts they had remained adamant in their refusal to let us in to their lives, and I couldn't help feeling that they had been right to do so. They didn't need to have recognised the true danger of the camera: just our being there had changed them. At least they had protected what they knew from what they did not. Yirus refused to be drawn further on the subject and we would never know what he had said to them but, as Bruce had guessed, it seemed likely he had been persuading them not to let us in for their own sakes. He was Korowai, after all, not of the same clan but one of them none the less.

After several hours of fast walking we met a group of young boys whose path converged with our own. They abandoned whatever they had set out to do in favour of the much more amusing spectacle of two white men falling off logs and our party was suddenly eleven. The three youngest of our new companions each carried a simple harpoon, consisting of a straight length of fencing wire with a short length of inner tube rubber - so that was what it was for - attached to one end and the other sharpened to a fine point. In addition, they each had a pair of well-used swimming goggles wrapped round an arm. 'For fish?' I imitated a fish-like motion with my hand.

'*Udang! Udang!*' They chorused.

'That means shrimp!' said Bruce, with surprise. 'They speak Indonesian!'

I rubbed my stomach. The boys' eyes widened and they laughed.

'Well, I think that's lunch sorted,' Bruce said, and set off in front of me.

We clambered down a bank and into the cool, clear, unruffled water of a river I didn't remember from yesterday's outward journey. A quick check with the compass identified it as flowing in the right direction, and the team waded down its middle. As the water slowed and deepened, the banks broadened into a lazy pool and the harpoonists fanned out along the shady bank, goggles on, glancing at us to be certain we were watching. I stopped in waist-deep water on the opposite side and opened the camera box on an exposed tree-trunk. An electric-blue dragonfly dipped its tail into the water just inches from me and smaller insects flitted about against the dark curtain of the opposite bank. It was hard to follow the hunters underwater with the camera. I wanted to shoot them surfacing with fat shrimps impaled on their harpoons, but could only just see their deft movements with the naked eye. 'Where's he gone? I can't see the middle one.'

Bruce gave directions. 'He's going right… right… now coming towards us…'

My quarry exploded from the water with a massive *udang* on the end of his harpoon. Within fifteen minutes four of the unfortunate creatures, each a good eight to ten inches long, were lined up on the tree-trunk but I had not captured one of the victorious surfacings. Bruce tried to orchestrate a staged repeat but the boys took this to mean we wanted more shrimp so we gave up in favour of having lunch at the fire, which had been lit, a few hundred yards downstream. Flung into the flames for just a few minutes, those *udang* were the most delicious I had ever eaten - the gastronomic experience of the expedition so far.

Just before nightfall the screech of insects gave way once more to the rush of water as we stepped out of the trees and on to the stones of the Eilanden river. To my delight Mr Homburg and Yalil were waiting there to ferry us home.

This time we made one diagonal downstream crossing and had an exciting ride through the powerful current, bailing out the incoming water as the paddlers strove to avoid dead trees that smashed the rolling surface of the water. As he balanced on the bucking prow Mr Homburg sang as he dug in his paddle. His song, which was somewhere between a birdcall and alpine yodelling, appeared to have something to do with staving off misfortune and blended beautifully with the rush of the water and Yalil's rhythmic grunting on the stern. I looked back at the wall of forest and wondered if we would get another chance in there further north. Porters or no porters, I couldn't see this river allowing us across again unless we found another canoe.

8 THE GAHARU TRADE

Throughout the evening Yirus could be heard stirring up dissent amongst the porters, and we went to bed knowing there would be trouble in the morning.

There was, and at one point the men were walking out of the clearing on their way home. Once again we capitulated to their demands. Superman was disheartened by the episode. I wondered if he knew more about Yirus's reasoning than he made apparent to Bruce and me, whether his presence with us as an Indonesian, arrogant and superior, was the root cause of our porters' discontent. Now we were stuck where we were for another day, and they would accompany us only as far as Sera Dala, two days away. If we even mentioned going back into the forest they would drop everything and leave us. Labalaba admitted that he wanted to come all the way but was unsure about leaving the others.

When the situation had calmed Bruce slumped down next to me on a log and rolled a cigarette.

'Well done, mate,' I said. 'At least we now know there's a village ahead.'

'Yeah, but I've just learnt it has an airstrip. There may be police too. Why the hell didn't Superman tell us about it before?' What Bruce was really annoyed about, however, was another day of enforced rest. We had progressed only two days' slow walk from Mabul and had less than three weeks remaining on our visas. That we would end up overstaying our welcome had never been in question, but every extra day spent on this expedition would raise the price of our repatriation. If we did not find some reliable porters soon, the crossing of the island would be beyond our budget.

That evening Mr Homburg hooked a fish roughly the size of a dog. We had it for supper while his young son, still speechless at our presence, thumbed through the photographs in the one book we still carried, never once turning it the right way up!

At first light we all filed out of the clearing. Mrs Homburg, as yet rarely seen and very shy with us, led the way to the start of the onward path with a small child we hadn't seen before, in a string bag hanging on her back. Second in the line was the boy, wielding and tripping over a *parang* that was almost as big as he was. Bruce tried to film the trio but Mrs Homburg shot off through the undergrowth whenever he got close to her. Superman led the remainder of the way along a fairly easy path rich in nutritional supplements. By midday each porter was carrying a leafy bundle of assorted frogs, insects and tobacco leaves. We had them for lunch.

That afternoon we waded between more islands until we reached the west bank of the river and stopped in another clearing, this time a tidy expanse of tall grass. A small stilted hut housed an unhealthy-looking family. We never got to the bottom of their relationship to each other, but I assumed the man in the torn Y-fronts with the emaciated left leg six inches shorter than the other was married to the girl with the swollen right leg wearing a grass skirt and grimy T-shirt with *'Alien Nation'* printed on the back. The old man in shorts, who took such an interest in the contents of my pack, had to be grandfather to the girl's small boy.

A bit further through the grass we found the skeletal remains of a much larger and distinctly un-Irianese dwelling.

'My hut,' announced Superman proudly. We looked at him quizzically. We knew little about Superman at this stage, other than that he had been an electrician in the Maluccas Islands and was now something to do with illegal logging. Whenever we had enquired he had been guarded as to his role in the latter. We sat him down on the remains of his balcony and interrogated him.

He had come up the river in a speedboat, he explained, and built this hut as one of his forward bases. From here he had sallied forth into the forest to recruit the indigenous locals to find a certain type of fragrant wood called *gaharu*. In return for the wood he gave them clothes, *parangs* and cooking pots. The wood was transported to Agats where it fetched a staggering $400 per kilo. The middlemen there shipped it to Jakarta where Chinese-incense-traders bought it for up to $1,000 per kilo. Bruce and I struggled with the irony: here we were, trying to overtake the tide of 'civilised' goods and influence sweeping through this forest and, as a guide, we had chosen one of the men responsible for its advance.

'So, before you came these people had no clothes or *parangs*?' Bruce asked.

'Oh, they had nothing!' Superman was smug.

I looked up at the naked rafters. 'How long ago were you here?'

'Almost two years ago. There was no more *gaharu* here so I had to go to a different area.'

Our expedition had just plummeted to the depths of eco-irresponsibility: we were practically sponsoring Superman's future exploitation of the forest, seeing him through a lean period. At this point Yirus informed us maliciously that he and his three stooges would come no further. They planned to return to their homes in the morning.

If he was expecting dismay he was to be disappointed. '*Bagus*. Good,' we chorused, and he turned away wearing a murderous expression.

'No problem, I will find more people here,' Superman assured us.

Labalaba was downcast at the idea of going home and we persuaded him to carry on without much difficulty. His eagerness to see more and have an adventure had endeared him to us, and what was more, he was an orphan who clearly deserved some fun. 'Yirus, bad man,' he said quietly. 'Bangol, Yalil and Laville, good men, but they are afraid.'

'Why are they afraid?' I asked.

'If you go back into the Korowai they will be eaten.'

'Are you afraid?'

'No.'

'Why are you not afraid?'

'With you and Mr Bruce the Korowai Khanum Khatun will be afraid.'

I wasn't convinced of that.

Despite lashing rain that began before we had finished our supper the atmosphere was lighter once we had paid off Yirus and Co. While they and Labalaba slept in the family's hut we bedded down beneath the floor of the ruined one. Bruce wanted to try out his bivi-bag and offered Superman his hammock and basha sheet. Now equipped with my luxurious sleeping-bag and Bruce's luxurious hammock there was no shutting him up. Purring sounds and cries of 'Oooh, *enaak*! Delicious!' accompanied every change of position. When I was sure he was asleep I loosened one of the guys on his basha sheet to let the heavy rainwater run in through his mosquito net.

In the morning Labalaba told us that the others had left early, before light. We soon discovered why: the section of blue awning we had bought from Mr Homburg for future porters and Superman's spare shirt were missing. His fury at waking up in a pool of water was now happily diverted to Laville who, according to Labalaba, was the culprit - for the shirt at least. From the gestures that followed I gathered that on his return to Binam he was going to go back up-river and punch Laville's lights out.

We approached the hut. Like it or not its occupants would have to be our porters and we'd recruit any neighbours as well. As Superman set off to search for others, it was clear that we had yet another day of indolence and sloth before us.

The next day, as everyone prepared to shoulder their loads, I looked at our new team and wondered if any of my boyhood heroes, such as Wilfred Thesiger, had gone about recruiting the sick and crippled, women and children to carry their loads. Could this be justified? What would people back home think? It would only be for a day, but still...

Superman saw me looking askance at the man with the

emaciated leg. 'No problem - strong.'

In fact, it was only the two healthy-looking young men Superman had found who complained about the weight. The family were in high spirits at the impending shopping trip: Sera Dala had a kiosk of sorts and they were about to make some money to spend in it. I needn't have worried about their load-carrying ability at all: the man with the bad leg set a respectable pace throughout the day, chattering noisily all the way.

At a rest stop we met a lone hunter. He jumped when he saw Bruce and me and looked about to flee until our new companions put him at ease. For the next fifteen minutes he never took his eyes off us.

By 4.30 p.m. we were close to the village so Bruce called a halt and led the way off the path and into some thick undergrowth. We would pay everyone except Labalaba now and send them ahead to check for a police presence. If the coast was clear, Superman and Labalaba would return with whoever they could find to carry the bags. As they left we camouflaged the entrance to our hiding-place and settled back to wait. Bruce took a reading from the GPS and I plotted it on the map. 'I thought we'd been going a bit too far north.' I showed him the position. We were miles away from the point that Superman had indicated as Sera Dala, miles away from our intended route and from the area we wanted to have another go at exploring. But it hardly mattered: our first priority was to find porters.

'What are your thoughts?' Bruce asked.

Although it was not part of the original plan, and we were running short of time, I wanted to have another attempt at interacting with the Korowai. We could leave all but the essentials in the village and make a lightweight trip back down to the river and beyond.

'So do I,' Bruce said. 'You're not hacked off that we've come a day's walk in the wrong direction, then?'

'No, we had to come here. It's the only village anyone seems to know about.'

'Ssh, someone's coming!'

We sat still and listened as a large group of people approached the hidden entrance to our mosquito-infested hole. As we held our breath, they turned sharp left and crashed into our position.

'Mr Mark, Mr Bruce, the police are here!' Superman called, amid much laughter. He had brought a gang of nine men with him, all native Irianese, no policemen. They were all burly-looking fellows.

I got to my feet and immediately wanted to sit down again. My right foot felt as if an incendiary device had gone off inside the boot. The remaining twenty-minute walk over slippery stones and criss-crossing a small river was depressingly painful. My boots were comfortable so it couldn't be blisters. I began to think something had bitten me.

Sera Dala is quite a modern-looking village of twenty dwellings arranged around a grass airstrip. One particularly flashy hut, complete with tin roof and real glass windows, was something to do with the Missionary Aviation Fellowship (MAF); it operated a handful of light aircraft and a helicopter in support of Irian Jaya's more remote missions. The last hut on the south-western side belonged to a man named Meruli, a Javanese acquaintance of Superman, who invited us to stay.

Meruli's home was his trading-post. He, too, was in the *gaharu* business, exchanging imported goods and food for tiny bundles of the precious wood as it was brought in by locals. He housed, clothed and fed three young local boys, orphans, who slept in his annexe and spent much of each day carving out, with hooked chisels, the undesirable whiter sections of the wood. Several times a day a new batch arrived wrapped in dry grass in traditional string bags. Processed wood was shipped out aboard the MAF aircraft that stopped here so infrequently, bringing in, among other cargo, fresh stocks of goods for barter. Our quietly spoken host explained that in a few years time, when he had amassed enough money, he would leave his monastic existence here in Irian Jaya and return to Java to find a wife. He was thirty-two.

That evening Meruli had a full house. Most of the men were from the village and spoke Kopka, but this was also our first meeting with people of the Una tribe, from the hills ahead of us. Physically they did not look much different from the lowlanders we had grown used to but their shorts and T-shirts were in better condition. Their association with Meruli and the *gaharu* trade had given them a cash crop.

Oil lamps threw warm light over the semi-circle of men facing us across the rough planks of the floor. The atmosphere was relaxed and friendly, without the crush and noise we had found in the Asmat villages and in Mabul. Meruli had invited them all to hear our plans and offer advice or help on the route ahead.

One man, Yanus, offered suggestions calmly and at a speed sympathetic to our grip of Indonesian. But the news was not good: no one would come with us if we chose to follow the river along the most direct route to the mountain. There were no villages and it was Korowai territory. 'Very dangerous,' Yanus concluded, and the man next to him mimed firing a bow and arrow.

'Khanum Khatun?'

The name triggered a spate of stories, but it was clear that, even here, little was known about them. None of these men knew exactly where they were, or were keen to find out. Unless we abandoned everything we couldn't carry ourselves we would have to find a new route to the mountain. Yanus suggested what looked like an enormous detour through the foothills and listed the villages we would find: Lukun, Bebecleh, Krabu and Kap Kap - all of the Una tribe.

So there were villages among the foothills ahead, but exactly where they lay, which valley Yanus meant - and even whether we were all talking about the same mountain - remained a mystery. We earmarked Yanus as a possible head porter, then explained that first we would head south again in search of the *Khanum Khutun*.

The next morning Labalaba left us. We decided that his change of heart was probably due to the conversation of the previous evening. Some of the men had graphically described the tough trails and cold that awaited us in the foothills, and in the clear morning air the hills were visible. It was the first time Labalaba had seen them. The forested slopes showed dark against the glare: a forbidding black wall broken only by solitary puffs of cloud manoeuvring between the peaks.

'Where is Mandala?' Lalalaba asked me, as I stood on the airstrip matching high points with the map. I took a bearing and guided his eyes to a perfectly conical hill of 10,000 feet that lay thirty miles to the north-east. He digested the information that the mountain was a long way beyond that – fifty-five miles in a straight line from where we stood - with a barely audible, *'Jau sekali*. Very far.'

9 LOOKING FOR CANNIBALS

The ground we covered that afternoon was familiar until its sudden unfamiliarity hinted that we had lost the path. No problem, we assured a distressed Superman, our destination lay along a more easterly bearing anyway: we'd make our own path. He accepted this but I could see that he was far from happy. He listened sullenly while Bruce instructed him on how to use a compass and to walk on a bearing. There was no argument as to who should lead the way and cut a path - despite the five-days' worth of dried rations and bananas he now carried, Superman's pack remained the size of a school satchel. Other evidence that this was a lightweight patrol was nowhere to be found: the satellite phone and personal kit I had left with Meruli had been replaced with a bag of gifts, a fifty-metre rope and a grappling-hook. My rucksack still weighed a ton, as did Bruce's. We set off again, anxious to cover a few more kilometres before dark. Superman warmed to his new skill and had cheered up by the time we stopped at the bank of one of the Eilanden's many unnamed tributaries where another, smaller river fed into it.

This was our first camp without the hubbub of porters or inquisitive onlookers, and it was bliss. With sleeping arrangements erected on the bank and out of a flash-flood's way, we cooked dried chicken and pasta on the shingled edge of the smaller river. Although the scene was similar to that of the Korowai camp of four nights previously it felt different here. There was an extra buzz of excitement. We were heading again into what felt like forbidden territory, but this time we had no locals with us. For once, nobody knew where we were. I looked around me into the starless night. Our little fire kept the shadows at bay, but barely. Cloaked in darkness, anything or anyone could have crept up on us and be watching from just a few feet away.

On the other side of the planet our own world would be bathed in light. You don't notice the dark so much in the developed world. There's always a light-bulb, a door, the glow of a nearby town, a car's headlights. Here, though, as the last flame died, the darkness rushed in. I was swimming in it, my skin tingling, every sense but sight magically enhanced. For a while no one spoke or moved. We listened to the clamour of insects and rushing water, smelt the decaying vegetation. Then Superman switched on a torch.

We were out of firewood and nobody could be bothered to find more. Superman and Bruce headed to their beds, the latter's torch beam chopping feebly at the night as he climbed the bank. I hadn't finished writing so lit a candle and lay on my roll-mat by the embers. Somewhere up-river it had been raining - the water was rising, creeping silently across the stones into the light. I kept watch on it out of the corner of my eye and packed up when it reached the end of my mat and the embers died with a hiss.

In contrast to the relaxed companionable evening, the next day was fraught with argument and frustration. Once we had waded across the tributary Superman lapsed into a sulk over our relatively slow progress through the swampy forest. He took to forging ahead without cutting a decent path for Bruce and me to manoeuvre along with our towering packs, frequently disappearing so far in front that we lost what little path he had made. Finally, having yet again relocated one another by a series of bizarre animal calls, we stopped him.

'I only know the way to Pondok Jon from my own hut,' he wailed.

'Where is Pondok Jon, and why do you want to go there?' Bruce asked, while I wandered about with the GPS held above my head, trying to pick up three or more satellites through the canopy.

It transpired that Bapak Jon, Mr Jon, was another *gaharu* merchant, and it had been near his *pondok*, or hut, that Superman had met the tribesmen he had told us about and to whom he wanted to take us. The real reason behind his discomfort soon became clear: he was no longer leading the way. Without following a known route he had no more idea of where he was than a storm-blown goose on the wrong side of the Atlantic. Yet his two charges were calmly instructing him in the use of a compass, confident that they knew exactly where they were going. I realised that until now he must have believed that Bruce and I were as useless in this environment as our boots. Suddenly he had plummeted from guide and saviour of the day to tawdry hanger-on. He could see his usefulness to us dwindling. It was also clear that he felt hard done by at being the one to cut the path. As my impatience with him grew, I concentrated on the GPS, leaving Bruce to reassure him that we still needed his help, but that he was not the boss.

For a while he co-operated, but it wasn't long before the strange animal calls were once again passing back and forth. I kept a check on our heading with my own compass and Superman was consistently too far to the west, still trying to lead us back to somewhere he might recognise. We began to cut our own path, ignoring his furious shouts, and discussed his future. Certainly he would have little to offer us later on in the mountains - unless he carried a decent load and we both knew there was no chance of that. We agreed that he must go, but not yet.

Shortly after four o'clock we were stopped in our tracks by a narrow but deep and powerful torrent, too dangerous to wade. A scout up and down the bank found no easy spot at which to cross and we elected to christen one of the grappling-hooks. We could see no sizeable trees above the head-high undergrowth on the far bank, which suggested an island prone to submerging in the wet season. The GPS confirmed that we had reached our old friend the Eilanden and, therefore, that this was probably just the first of many channels. The hook caught on a decent anchor point on the fifth throw but by the time the ropework was ready there was daylight left only for a quick reconnaissance to the other side of the island. Meanwhile a huge storm cloud had parked maliciously overhead. The treetops lashed about wildly in its updraught and as I made the crossing it unleashed a startling clap of thunder. The rope was either too slack or not high enough to keep me above the water and I had to pull myself sideways through the current, surfing on my chest to avoid being forced under. The rain was so heavy it all but cut off any remaining light. Behind Bruce I could just make out Superman rushing to erect one of the basha sheets as I dismantled the improvised harness round my waist.

The island took only five minutes to cross but as I pushed my way through the tall grass I felt an unexpected and powerful fear come over me. I was in the middle of a vast river, visibly and audibly cut off from the assumed safety of my friends, and the water level was rising. On the other side I could see the network of channels and islands that lay ahead but there was no sign of any tall trees marking the far bank through the turmoil of water in the air. The thunder, rain and rushing water deafened me to everything but the thump of my heart. I felt naked and vulnerable. The tall grass and scrub I had pushed through wore an odd greyish translucence as the wind whipped it into life around me to grab at my legs with serrated edges. I had to control an urge to run, then found the fear replaced with excitement.

By the time I was standing on safe ground again, Bruce was already sitting in the shelter of the basha sheet, puffing at a cigarette. He filmed Superman and me erecting the other shelter.

When we awoke the localised storm had done little with the water level. It still took the entire day to reach the safety of the eastern bank and all three of us nearly died in the process. We forded nineteen separate watercourses, using a variety of techniques and breaking every rule in the book. Most were wadeable with a stout stick and great care, but their width rendered the use of a rope, even as a safety-line, impractical. Loss of footing offered almost certain entrapment against lethal-looking tangles of dead wood that stuck out of the water and from the banks everywhere we looked.

The thirteenth torrent took over four hours to cross as we tried in vain to get a grappling-hook into a pile of wood forced against the upstream point of the next island. We were on a tiny shingle island and could just wade in to what looked like a throwable distance. But Bruce, by far the best of us at throwing a coiled rope, could not quite manage it and grew more tired at each attempt. I was in favour of searching for another spot. Superman insisted on having a go from a position further into the current. His throw was even more pathetic than my efforts and no sooner had the grappling-hook left his hand than he was swept away. He returned to us some fifteen minutes later, still shaking.

In the end, bravely or foolishly, Bruce strode to the upstream edge of our island, took a running dive and swam across with the rope end, just making the other side before getting to the end of the coil. We swung the first rucksack across but should have used two ropes joined end to end: in order for Bruce to reach it, Superman and I had to wade waist deep into the current. It took every ounce of our strength for us to remain upright on the loose stones underfoot, whilst Bruce unclipped the rucksack, then fight our way back on to the island, the rope kicking and straining against us. Unfortunately the second rope had gone across in the first bag, but buoyed by success we ignored the difficulties and set about the second rucksack.

Further into the current than Superman, I felt the stones beneath my feet shift and realised I was about to be swept away. Superman's face showed the strain as he struggled with the rope end, his feet ploughing through the stones as the current grabbed me.

'*Tidak! Tidak!*' I screamed at him to let go of the rope. If he came across too we would have a hell of a time retrieving the camera boxes and his own bag. He let go and the river swept me away.

I felt no panic. I expected merely to pendulum across and thought I would be able to surf on my chest when the rope reached full stretch. But in mid-stream this fancy was shattered when, with a sudden jerk, the tautened rope yanked me violently beneath the surface. I hung on grimly while the water buffeted me from side to side and the rope tore at my hands, but had to let go, tumbling with the current and struggling to find air. On surfacing I struck out for the far bank. Now there was panic: through the adrenaline rush I was keenly aware of what lay in store if I did not make it before the island ran out. Downstream loomed the next tangled, foaming death trap. I knew that if the current rammed me into that I would be lucky to escape. I swam like a madman. A brief moment of indecision as to whether I should try the other direction was mercifully quashed and I found myself in the safety of an eddy.

Standing on the bank I waited for my heartrate to slow, then joined Bruce in the new struggle to get the rope back across to Superman. From the elevated platform of this island it was easier, and we had soon pulled across the remaining kit, with Superman.

The day wore on until there was one large crossing left between us and a line of tall trees that marked the end of the ordeal. Tempers had frayed, and Bruce and I were exchanging our first angry words of the trip when a man appeared on the other side. He seemed to be pointing us further upstream, disappearing frequently into the long grass then stopping at what certainly appeared to be a better spot. It was comparatively narrow, with a favourable bend, and we set about crossing it with the vigour that comes from knowing that an ordeal is almost over. The current and depth were too much for my fatigued legs, though, and I became stuck midway across. The rock supporting my downstream boot was moving and I had no choice but to swing off my pack and dive after it. Superman ran back into the current to try to catch me but I found it surprisingly easy now. This was a much less exhausting method of crossing if you could afford to be swept downstream a little. Scrambling, slipping, swimming, kicking and bouncing, I dragged my luggage to the bank and raised two fingers defiantly at the river.

We had been going for almost eleven hours without a break, and the GPS showed that we had travelled only 1,200 metres since the previous night's camp. We were back in Korowai territory.

The man on the bank had what looked like half a walnut shell lashed to the end of his penis. He spoke no Indonesian but we got along fine with tobacco and sign language. He led us to three huts he called Kowet, just half an hour into the forest. One of the younger men there spoke some Indonesian and introduced himself as Yakop, but none of us had much energy for chit-chat. Bruce and Superman slept in his hut. I strung my hammock between two of the stilts supporting it and found myself directly under the fireplace. It was not alight but every footstep in the room above sent a shower of fine ash through my mosquito net. I could not have cared less. Any spare emotion was occupied with the doctoring of my right foot. It had swollen, was largely devoid of skin and rotten. The pain I had felt in it since we had entered Sera Dala was now explained: I had 'immersion foot', a variation of trench foot. I rammed lumps of cotton wool soaked in antiseptic between my toes to prevent the raw flesh sticking together, and swallowed some dyhydrocodeine painkillers. Why only my right foot had succumbed to this debilitating condition was a mystery.

Over breakfast Superman was in high spirits. Yakop not only knew of Bapak Jon's *pondok* but would lead us there by a path. We were unable to ascertain to which tribe he and his cohabitants at Kowet belonged but he was adamant that he would not risk going further south than Pondok Jon. His knowledge of that area matched Superman's: that there was a small river further south beyond whose banks lived the Khanum Khatun in the east and the Batu in the west. He and three others would use this opportunity to search for wild pig. Superman chose this moment to reveal that he had another hut, which lay on the bank of this unmarked river.

I put on my boots. My foot felt grim. I had been dreading standing up with my pack on. The first two hundred metres out of Kowet were along a series of connecting log walkways. These would be difficult to balance on at the best of times, and despite having taken more codeine I was limping heavily. The pack on my back swung wildly about with each lurch and balancing was impossible. Before the end of the first log I had fallen off into the undergrowth three times. When Superman offered to swap loads

I didn't argue.

That Pondok Jon, when we reached it after a long day's walk, still had a roof was probably due to its not infrequent use by Yakop and others as a forward base for their pig-hunting exploits. We arrived just in time to make good use of it under yet more torrential rain. Yakop was still firm in his resolve not to accompany us any further south but Superman assured us that he knew the way to his own hut on the river not two hours away. For forty minutes we followed him with flagging optimism as we trudged around in little circles in search of 'the path'. Finally my feet could take no more and, ignoring his protests, we fixed a bearing with the GPS, cutting a straight line back to Yakop in less than fifteen minutes.

We spent the evening giving our new companions a geography lesson on the inflatable globe and patching up our feet and leg sores. Due to our half-hourly falls Bruce and I both sported a spectacular array of cuts and stab wounds that had all turned into suppurating tropical ulcers. Our companions' wounds were mostly old ones but while slow to heal they seemed not to have the same problems with infection – well-adapted immune systems, no doubt. We doled out antiseptic solution generously, however, and I took a sadistic pleasure in directing a spray of tincture of benzine into a nasty-looking cut that Yakop had acquired that day on his foot. Tough as these men were, he flinched at the infamous 'tinc-benz', and at the sight of his distress all further wounds for our attention were swiftly hidden. Bruce's feet were deteriorating along the same lines as mine, and even, I admitted grudgingly, looking worse. His raw patches had not yet joined up but they went further than mine, reaching his ankles and beyond.

Yakop showed Superman where he had gone wrong the previous evening and we made the ruins of our trusty guide's second hut in time for a late breakfast. It was a skeleton but for the bark floor, and the little river ran past just a few feet away. It was the northern boundary of the area, that from all the scraps of information we had accumulated since paddling into the village of

Karabis two weeks before, seemed to be the most likely in which to encounter some truly 'untouched' people. Here, we reckoned we stood a good chance of hitting human tracks that might lead to a settlement. We had constantly debated how we wanted to play this, what we wanted to achieve, and the moral implications of what we were about to do. We had already filmed people without their understanding of what we were doing. Where was the line between responsible respect for their privacy and outright exploitation? Neither of us wanted to answer that: our curiosity had become too powerful. We would find what we could in the small amount of time available to us, and film everything, but if our subjects were unreceptive we would leave. Furthermore, in any future reference to the event, written or broadcast, we would deliberately mislead anyone intending to follow in our footsteps as to the area, its location and our own route to it.

Back in London we had envisaged the possible scenario of us stepping out of the trees and into an inhabited clearing and had wondered how we might film such a meeting without alarming people or distracting them with the main camera. The solution came in the form of a tiny lens the size of a miniature bottle of spirits. Wired up to the main camera via a control box this clever little device, with its built-in microphone, more commonly used for such purposes as to film a Grand Prix from the driver's viewpoint, fitted neatly on to the peak of a baseball cap. The main camera could then be carried out of sight either in the top of the cameraman's rucksack or in a bum-bag. The difficulty with this set-up, however, was keeping the lens pointing in the same direction as the cap-wearer's eyes, and the lack of rigidity inherent in the baseball cap. In previous trials we had also found that any movement of the main camera within its hiding-place had a tendency to switch it off. As the sun burnt off the last of the cloud above Superman's old hut and fed the solar panels arranged across its floor, we spent almost an hour trying to get it right. I practised the head movement to keep whatever I looked at central in the screen while Bruce struggled with the storage problem. But we might as well not have bothered: as I climbed out of the river and up the far bank a sound problem announced itself in the earphones and we abandoned the idea in favour of getting a move on.

Almost at once we came across an obvious path winding in a south-easterly direction. A short while later it split into two and we opted for the more trodden fork. We felt as if we were on a hunt, creeping along the path, speaking in low tones. The sense of trepidation and excitement was intense, despite the pleasantly relaxing narcotic effect of the codeine that Bruce and I had taken before setting off. Superman, wearing a pair of plastic shoes he had bought in Sera Dala, had developed a raw patch beneath his right ankle, and was becoming increasingly anxious as we ventured along the track, so we gave him one of the pills, and popped another each for good measure. He quietened right down and trotting after us looking rather glazed.

As more and more junctions presented themselves we based our choice of path on direction: we did not want to head west and end up in Batu territory so tried to maintain a general east-south-east bearing. It was all but impossible. Many paths were dead ends, stopping abruptly against a solid wall of foliage. Others bore tantalising human footprints but twisted and turned until we were going in the wrong direction, then either disappeared or became barely discernible trails. Most exciting was the lack of a clean cut on every sapling and small tree that had been felled: each had been crudely chopped with many blows from a blunt edge rather than the efficient slice of a steel blade. Stone axes.

But the day wore on without any human sounds or conclusive evidence that we were not wandering up the 'garden path'. The drug wore off too. I knew Superman was clear-headed when he sat down at one of the junctions and complained about the pain in his shoulders. I took back my pack and thanked him for his help.

Towards late afternoon, in an area dotted with swampy stands of *sago* palms, we finally stumbled upon a tall treehouse, standing on ten-metre legs at the edge of a small clearing. In a flurry of excitement we prepared the camera, then called out the greeting

Labalaba had taught us. '*Atei...atei!* Father...father!'

There was no one at home, and no smoke to indicate the usual fire kept ticking over. We elected to wait among the five stilts in the hope that it was a home rather than a remote *sago*-gathering outpost. By five thirty when no one had appeared I felt it was safe to climb the ladder and have a look inside. It was in good condition with patches of new bark flooring but the fire had not seen any recent action. Bones and skulls from small mammals and birds, remnants of past meals, poked out from the underside of the thatch in a manner we had grown used to, but there was no sign of any belongings or weaponry. I poked my head out to report down to Bruce and was in mid-sentence when I noticed another roof, at a much lower altitude, not twenty metres away over a belt of secondary growth.

Other than the path by which we had approached there was just one other, a narrow avenue between high bushes, and it went in the right direction. I took the small camcorder on a reconnaissance mission. At first it appeared to be another cul-de-sac but at the end of an old log there was a small opening in the bushes, just big enough to crawl through. On the other side the hut was brand new, not quite finished. Strips of fresh bark lay discarded on the ground, but no builders. Throughout the evening we thought we could hear voices not far away. We kept quiet: we did not want to attract attention to ourselves and be surprised in our sleep. In the morning we would investigate. Later, as I lay in my hammock, I realised I had left my diary at Pondok Jon.

Next morning, the first up, I lit a small fire for a mug of hot water and was just lighting a cigarette when I heard a rustling along the path towards the other hut. I stood stock still. 'Bruce! Superman!' I hissed at their recumbent forms. There wasn't time to wake them: I could see the undergrowth moving. Whoever was coming was just feet away. I tried to remember the Korowai greeting but my mind was blank.

The face of a teenage girl appeared above the grass. At first she didn't notice me and I called the Indonesian greeting to her. '*Selamat!*'

She froze, head and shoulders framed by the vivid green. Our eyes met, hers widened in alarm, and she fled. Instinctively, my hand went to my beard and then to my dishevelled hair. I must look horrifying, I thought. Whatever, others would know now of our trespass and we could expect a visitation.

Bruce and Superman tumbled out of bed. We packed our hammocks and any other loose bits of kit and sat down to wait, cameras at the ready. A good half-hour passed before a cacophony of rustling and male voices announced the imminent arrival of a large group by the same path - an armed party to chase us away, perhaps, or someone as yet unaware of our presence. Before any faces appeared we called, '*Atei!*' as the cameras started turning.

A shock of frizzy hair appeared above the grass, then a man's face, unafraid, not aggressive. Suddenly our little clearing was full of people, men and boys. All but four were clothed in shorts and T-shirts and several of the men carried *parangs*. I lowered the camera in disappointment. They were Kopka men, from a village well to the north, prospecting for *gaharu*. They had a few Korowai Batu with them, one of whom was the youth I had mistaken for a girl. They told us that we must go further east to find the Khanum Khatun and that, no, they would not go there.

'*Tidak bisa masuk.* You cannot enter,' said their leader.

We lost no time in setting off again, ignoring footprints, taking only the paths that led us through the labyrinth in an east-north-easterly direction, hacking our way through the jungle when they turned the wrong way or stopped altogether, until we found another.

We went as fast as we could. The search was taking too long: we were running out of food and seemed to be going round in circles. As the morning passed, footprints and recognisable paths became scarcer and scarcer. Did these people really exist? I asked myself. Since re-entering the Korowai area we had seen more people wearing clothes than not. Perhaps the Westernisation brought in by the *gaharu* traders and missionaries had covered the whole region now and the Khanum Khatun were just a myth. If they did exist perhaps they would not allow themselves to be found by three idiots barging through the jungle. I looked around me at the thick vegetation: we could walk past a barn in this stuff and not see it. All a group of people would have to do to avoid us was keep quiet - and as hunters they were experts at that.

Suddenly we heard cooing and wailing noises and froze, straining to hear more between ominous rumbles of thunder rolling over the canopy far above us, until the roar of a million raindrops hitting a million leaves drowned everything. They won't be able to hear us coming in this, I thought, as we headed carefully in the direction of the sounds we had heard. Despite the din of the storm we spoke in whispers and moved silently, careful not to snap twigs or branches. I felt like a soldier in Belize again, on a patrol along the Guatemalan border, then remembered how easy it was to ambush someone in the jungle. My mind wandered back to that horrible arrow designed for men.

An hour passed and, as suddenly as it had started, the rain stopped. We halted to take stock of the situation. There was nothing for it but to keep going and I set off again. Behind me I heard Bruce whisper, 'Superman, *senang?* Happy?'

There was no answer but I heard Bruce trying to suppress a giggle. He was loving this and, I had to admit it, so was I. The excitement was intense. In my wildest dreams I had never thought to experience such a feeling of exploration, such a thrill at the unknown. Every sense I possessed felt as highly-tuned as it could possibly be. My ears picked up the slightest tremor of sound – a seed falling to the ground, a far-off birdcall, the rustle of ants swarming up a nearby tree-trunk. My eyes darted between the tiniest movements in the undergrowth. My nose relished the heady scents emerging after the rain.

'Sssh!' Bruce's urgent whisper stopped me in my tracks but I had heard it too – muffled voices ahead, very close. We took a few steps further and realised the forest was about to give way to a clearing. Peering through the remaining trees I could just see the roof of another treehouse. My eyes dropped to scan the ground beneath it. Where were they? In the treehouse or right in front? Another muffled voice. They were inside.

Were these the Khanum Khatun? Bruce was slipping a new cassette into his camera. I had forgotten about the camera in my hands and fumbled with it for a second – battery good, cassette good.

We composed ourselves, then walked steadily into the clearing, Superman calling out the usual greeting as we covered the last few yards. The cameras were on but neither of us was ready for what followed.

10 THE KHANUM KHATUN

No sooner had Superman called out his greeting than pandemonium broke out in the treehouse. Cries of alarm shattered the forest calm. A man rushed out of the doorway and made as if to escape down the crude ladder but at the sight of us advancing though the bushes he stopped in his tracks. Clinging to the ladder, he shrank into a ball as if he was trying to hide, cowering, his eyes wide with fear. A second, older man stepped out and stood against the wall staring down at us. A third, crouching submissively in the darkness of the doorway, alternately held his head and pointed to the sky, repeating the same cry, '*Owh, owh!*' From within the hut I could hear the shrill alarm of women.

Transfixed by the scene above, the three of us bumped into each other and stopped amid the bushes, just five metres from the structure's legs. This was what we had come for, yet we had no idea how to approach people who appeared terrified of us but were unable to run away. Our discussions on how we might play this had always revolved around the idea that we would step out of the forest and into a village scene. Now I realised that if we had, the people would have fled into the trees and we would not have seen them again. But these men were trapped, eight metres from the ground. Tentatively we advanced a few steps closer.

Renewed panic struck the men above us. '*Owh, owh!*' The man on the ladder seemed unsure where to go, what to do. He started to climb back to the ledge but stopped and cowered again, snatching terrified glances at us from behind the arm held protectively over his head.

'*Owh, owh!*' The third man was outside now, squatting just in front of the doorway. Repeatedly he made the same gesture

– throwing an open hand up to the sky then placing it back on his head as if to say, 'No! No! The sky will fall on our heads!'

While Bruce and Superman rummaged around for gifts to offer I concentrated on the scene before me. Only the oldest of the three men seemed to show no fear. He had remained silent so far, standing on the ledge of flooring that ran the width of the treehouse like a veranda and staring balefully at us. He wore only a strip of rattan around his waist and another slung across his chest. The man on the ladder was similarly dressed but with a strip of rattan round his left biceps and a bright necklace of pigs' teeth. The man squatting by the door seemed unadorned with anything. They seemed much darker-skinned than the clan we had met before but as they were standing in shadow I couldn't be sure.

'Mr Mark, Mr Bruce!' Superman's voice dragged my attention away from the men. He was on his knees and also covering his head and pointing to the sky, replicating their actions and indicating that we should do likewise. We both dropped down, patting our heads and lowering our eyes submissively.

'Mr Bruce, *di atas dulu, di atas dulu!* The sky first!'

'Oh, oh!' I mimicked their cries, pointed to the sky then tapped my head with one hand and tried to keep the camera steady on my knees with the other. I heard the auto-focus whirring as it struggled with the leaves now partially obscuring my view.

Bruce rose to his feet, dropped his rucksack and advanced a little further, holding up some bead necklaces.

'Owh, owh, owh!' All three men recoiled. The third retreated inside the hut. The old man started to follow him, then stood his ground. The third man came out again.

There was no sign of the situation calming. With our white skin, our clothes, the rucksacks like huge humps on our backs and the strange-looking cameras in our hands we must have appeared like nothing these people had even conceived of before we invaded their clearing. Their universe was the Korowai, a territory of swamp and forest only eighty kilometres long by forty kilometres wide, a micro-cosmos surrounded by six different tribes speaking six different languages. What lay outside their reality lived only in myth. Did our white skin indicate to them that we were spirits of the dead, as the Asmat people were known to have believed? Thank God we were not wearing sunglasses.

I felt incredibly uncomfortable. The excitement had left me. This was wrong. We had no right to be here. We were invaders, no better than paparazzi, trampling on these people's privacy for a story. For hundreds of years they and their ancestors had remained hidden from the outside world. And now we had turned up, ending their seclusion. We had brought them the first step towards destruction.

Kneeling there in the grass I felt is if I were in trance. It seemed as if I hadn't moved a muscle for an age yet I was still patting my head like an automaton, smiling up at them disarmingly and occasionally glancing down at the camera's side screen to ensure that I still had them in the frame. In a daze, I dragged my stare from the terrified men. Bruce was still five metres to my right, standing in clearer ground, offering gifts. Superman was on his knees just next to me, delving inside the gift bag for some more necklaces and intermittently wailing and bowing submissively. The whole scene was the most surreal of my life and I didn't know what to do.

The older man edged backwards through the doorway. Then the man on the ladder followed, still cowering and protecting his head. Lastly, the third man backed inside, never taking his eyes from mine. The '*Owh owh*' cries stopped. I could just see their shadowy forms moving in the darkness beyond the doorway but the foliage in front of me was in the way. In the sudden silence I could think more clearly. What were they doing? The *kepala desa* of Karabis had made similar sounds when describing the encircling hunt but there was no atmosphere of aggression here. Had they realised we meant them no harm? As I clung to that hope my unease vanished. I stood up to join Bruce for a better view and concentrated on filming what he was doing. Without turning his head he spoke urgently as I stepped out from the bushes.

'He's got his bow and arrow!'

A frenzied argument sounded from within the treehouse. We were just a few metres from the bottom of the ladder. I focused on the camera I still held at waist level and zoomed in on the glimpses of movement beyond the doorway above but couldn't see the weapon. The top of the ladder was in the way.

'Ok, ok!' Bruce jumped back suddenly, almost tripping on the tangled ground as he stepped past me and back into the cover of the bushes. 'Let's get out, mate!'

My feet were moving before I had fully registered what was going on. I hadn't seen what Bruce had – that just inside the doorway one of the men had drawn back an arrow and was about to fire. I just knew we were in danger. Bruce would not have given up on this unless we were about to be shot. Superman was still on his knees, oblivious to the danger and still calling out to them in Indonesian, which they clearly didn't speak. Bruce filled him in on the situation: '*Tingal disanna, pulang! Tingal disanna, pulang!* Leave it there! Let's go!'

I kept my eye on the treehouse as Bruce swung his rucksack on to his shoulders and Superman finished laying out beads and tobacco on a leaf on the ground, then we all headed back out of the clearing.

Before we had gone five paces a fresh outbreak of cries made us turn. The three men were back outside the doorway, pointing down at our offerings on the ground with open palms, as if pushing them away. They were unarmed but the message was clear: they wanted nothing we had. Bruce returned to the gifts and swept them up. The mens' cries followed us into forest.

'He was drawing his bow - did you see? There was an arrow pointing at me for a second,' Bruce said, as we marched between the trees.

I said nothing. I couldn't get over what had just happened. My head was spinning with a jumble of images, sounds and emotions I couldn't make sense of.

The guilt I had felt just a few minutes before was gone. In its place was wonderment. We were in the twenty-first century and had made first contact with a new group of human beings! Of that much I was certain. It wasn't just that they hadn't seen white people before: Bruce had asked that question of virtually everyone he had met since leaving Mabul and the answer was always 'No.' I was convinced that these men had never even seen an Indonesian face before, and perhaps had not even heard of white people. Not in my wildest, most adventurous childhood dreams had I ever imagined such a possibility. I knew that, technically, we hadn't discovered anything – it was already known that people lived there – but that wasn't the point. To me, it was a discovery. Suddenly the earth had changed for me: it was now refreshed, made even more remarkable somehow. There wasn't supposed to be anything like this left. Before leaving London, Bruce had contacted a leading anthropologist to ask how we should deal with a first contact. He had shrugged us off with the comment that such ideas were merely 'popular romantic notions' because there were no longer any uncontacted peoples.

But there was disappointment too. We still did not know anything about these people. I wanted desperately to share a day of their lives and it didn't look as if that was going to be possible.

On reaching a junction less than two hundred metres from the treehouse we stopped to decide what to do next. We couldn't pursue this encounter any further. The question now was whether we should head back to Sera Dala or have one last attempt even further eastwards. I was in two minds, stung once more by guilt yet now even more curious. Perhaps if we were to meet some other people - not like this, but on a path where they might not feel trapped and vulnerable: at least then they would have choice. If they ran away, so be it, but if they felt they had the upper hand they might be guided by their own curiosity. Any damage we had done by invading that last clearing seemed even worse because we still knew nothing about its inhabitants. Suddenly it seemed important to make good our intrusion.

Sitting on a fallen tree and poring over the map with Bruce, I rationalised that if we brought back something educational with our film, something that might even help the Korowai in the future, the damage might have been worthwhile.

Bruce looked irritated by my ceaseless meanderings around the moral issues. 'You seem to forget that we're only a few miles in front of the *gaharu* traders. They're the ones who are changing these people.'

A noise made us sit bolt upright. The howl of a dog sounded through the trees in the direction from which we had just come.

'That's a dog left alone. They must have left the treehouse,' I said warily.

Bruce nodded. 'They've probably gone to warn others. I don't think they'll come after us. Do you?'

'No.' Given their reaction to us, I thought that was the last thing they would do.

I was wrong. Voices drifted through the foliage towards us. We were being followed.

Bruce scrambled to his feet and whispered to Superman to get out some tobacco. I looked at my pack, undecided whether or not to put it on. Neither Bruce nor Superman had theirs on and the Korowai were making no effort to be silent. It did not sound as if they were hunting us. Instead I picked up the camera.

When our pursuers seemed to be just round the corner we called out to let them know we were there. We didn't want anyone loosing-off an arrow in panic.

'*Owh, owh, owh!*' The same cries rang out again and I realised they were already within ten metres of us, so close I should have been able to see them. I scanned the undergrowth until a movement in the leaves gave away their position; three faces barely visible amid the greenery.

The two younger men advanced a little and, with relief, I saw that they were not carrying any weapons, only string bags slung round their shoulders. We relaxed.

Bruce took a few steps towards them but stopped when the cries intensified. Their gestures and body language were unchanged: open palms thrust towards the sky and us, then withdrawn to cover and pat the head. This time, however, they seemed also to be pointing us towards a specific direction, imploring us to follow the path leading to the north-west. In front of me Bruce made a display of having understood and of our compliance. Then we shouldered our packs and set off down the path they had indicated. Behind us the Khanum Khatun fell silent and when I snatched a final glance over my shoulder they were gone. We did not stop walking again for twenty minutes.

All I could think about was the arrow. Barely concentrating on where my feet were falling I realised with a jolt that the only reason they had not fired was that they had been too afraid to do so. Even after it had dawned on them that we were not going to attack, they had been afraid of the consequences. In the aftermath of our retreat I had thought that they were threatening us to make us leave, but now I remembered the frenzied voices beyond that doorway. That was what they had been arguing about, I was sure: they had wanted to kill us but they weren't sure what would happen if they did. At least one had been ready to go for it but the others had stopped him.

'Why? They don't have any reason to fear the police.' Bruce spoke between heavy breaths - Superman was setting a frantic pace in front.

'That's not what I mean. I don't think they recognise any law that we know of. I think they thought something catastrophic might happen.'

'What? Like the sky falling on their heads?'

'Something like that - they might have thought we were ghosts. I reckon they did actually want to kill us.'

Bruce stopped suddenly. 'Mate, believe me, I was aware of that.'

'Well, the arrow was pointing at you, not me. I didn't even see it.'

Long after the first contact with the Korowai in 1978, Johannes Veldhuizen, the missionary responsible, learnt from the tribes people how they had viewed their first meeting. The people of the Sendekh clan had been slaughtering a pig on a riverbank when he had appeared in a canoe accompanied by men from a neighbouring tribe. They had thought the white man was a *laleo*, a bad spirit, and had fled. He had left gifts and departed. In the following weeks, while Veldhuizen repeated the process, a fierce debate raged among the Korowai. Some thought that the only way to save the universe from collapse was to kill the bad spirit, others that that the sky would surely fall if they did. At no point in the account is there mention of what they would do with the corpse of such a spirit. Cannibalism appears in other accounts of Korowai life documented by the missionaries, but only in the context of punishing *kakhua*, male witches. The Korowai have an 'obsessive fear' of the sorcery that is 'very often' blamed for natural deaths and use an elaborate system of investigation to discover who has fired the 'invisible arrow', or magically eaten the vital organs of the victim. The accused is executed, baked, and eaten.

The stories we heard all along the river are another viewpoint, but if the Khanum Khatun were afraid that our deaths would turn the world upside down I do not believe that Bruce and I would have been eaten. Superman might not have been so lucky though, and our porters' fear was justifiable.

At a small stream we halted to fill our water-bottles, fix a satellite position and assess our options. It had taken us a long time to get to this point in our journey. We were still three or four days' walk from the rest of our equipment and had all but run out of food. Our feet were rotten, and on two bananas a day I was feeling weak. The thought of having to cross the Eilanden again filled me with dread, yet cross it we must, and soon. There seemed to be more and more rain falling each day. If we became trapped in the Korowai by the rising river our only option for regaining our equipment would be to cut a path back to Mabul where the river was wider and slower and there were canoes. Mr Homburg's dugout was nearer but he might not hear our hail across the rushing water. In the meantime there were only eleven days left on our visas, and we were barely half-way to the mountain. It was time to get back on track. On the other hand, we had to have one last attempt at interaction with the people here. Just one night in their company would be enough to get a flavour of their lives.

We knew we should head back to Sera Dala, but thought we should still have another shot at it in another place, without the cameras and rucksacks. We agreed to keep going in an easterly direction but with a northerly bias that would eventually take us back to the river, which we could then follow back to the ruined *pondok*. Over the course of the next few hours we came across several more huts, but they were all deserted and offered no clues. Perhaps word had spread. Whatever the case, the river appeared sooner than we expected and we made to follow it back to Superman's hut. No path followed the banks so it was easier to walk down the middle. Easier still, I found, was to float my pack, walking and swimming beside it.

Despite the disappointment of having been turned away by the Khunum Khatun we were all in high spirits. We had proved to ourselves that something extraordinary was going on in these forests. It wasn't just riverbank gossip and hearsay: there were people who were 'uncontacted' by the outside world. We had only met what must have been a family group but I was still reeling at the memory of the encounter. Their reaction to us left me in no doubt that no one, not even a missionary or a *gaharu* trader, had been in that part of the forest before. These were certainly not the same people Superman had met: we had gone further than either he or Bapak Jon ever had. We had crossed from the known to the unknown, and there were humans on the other side.

That night we had a visitor, a silent prowler who walked among us as we slept. Bruce asked over breakfast - a banana each and a spoonful of chicken pasta for flavouring - if Superman or I had heard something moving about in the night. We hadn't, and were forty minutes' walk away, examining a felled tree mutilated for *gaharu*, when Bruce discovered that his *parang* was missing. We went back to search for it but without success. He was upset. It had been fashioned from a truck-spring for him by a Dayak tribesman in Borneo. When we reached Pondok Jon I had a look for my diary but it was not there. Yakop must have taken it with him.

The episode left us little time to make Kowet before dark and the afternoon became a long, hard slog. My foot gave me more grief than the codeine seemed able to cope with and I knew Bruce had the same problem, although he never complained. We were all relieved to reach Kowet just as darkness obscured the path, but Yakop had not yet returned.

We spent the next day waiting for my diary to turn up, but the wild pigs were evidently proving elusive. We bought a bunch of green bananas from an ancient man bedecked in boar's tusks but had no water to wash them down. Undaunted by our lack of enthusiasm the old man kept returning with more and bigger bunches. I begged him to take them away. If they had had even a hint of flavour I would gladly have suffered the fifteen-minute hobble to the nearest stream for some water, but they did not. The only thing to do was sit very still and not tax the brain so that starvation set in only slowly. We watched the solar panels charge the batteries. With various bits of wood that were lying around I made an aeroplane weathervane with a propeller that would spin in the wind.

I couldn't subject Bruce to another day of this, not with the remainder of our food only two days' march away, so in the morning we decided to move. There was still a chance that Yakop might follow us in the certain knowledge that the return of my book would yield a reward. A powerful-looking man called Yunis agreed to guide us across the Eilanden river and back to Sera Dala, but only for an exorbitant price. Superman silenced my protest with a wink and instructed me to hand over half of the requested sum. I must have looked perplexed, then had to hide a grin. Yunis could neither read nor count. He knew the names of large banknotes, but not what they looked like. We all smiled benignly at each other as he happily tucked the notes into his shorts. The guilt - a twinge - came when he proved his worth by leading us to a fording point that made our previous choice of crossing-place look like a section of the Amazon delta. Of course, we still faced the same volume of water but here, just half a mile upstream, there was no sign of white water. Nevertheless, it still looked exhausting.

Bruce ran into trouble between the fifth and sixth islands. Attempting to take the rope across while I filmed, he made it about two-thirds of the way before the drag of the rope lying across the swift current behind pulled him off his feet and began to swing him back to our side. Superman paid it out as slowly as he could without dragging Bruce under but still reached the bottom of the coil before Bruce had reached safe ground. The rope snapped taut against its anchor of rocks, sending a spray of droplets into the air along its length and Bruce was yanked beneath the water. He was only chest deep and had a loose loop around his shoulders, requiring just a twist of the body to escape, so I wasn't concerned for his safety.

I only knew how exhausting his experience had been when he rejoined us and I saw his face close up. He was pale and shocked, breathing heavily and moving with lethargic sluggishness. 'I felt I was going there,' he mumbled. 'I couldn't get the rope off, or stay on my feet. I'm not doing that again. I've never felt so knackered.'

I certainly wasn't going to try it - I had proved to myself that that method didn't work during the first crossing a week before. I had a better idea. 'We should do it like my crossing of the last section last time – go with the current rather than fight it, dragging our packs. Sod the rope.'

At that moment Yunis hoisted my rucksack on top of his head and ran into the water, yelling. The three of us just stared. His musical whooping grew muffled as the current swept him downstream and seemed to rise by an octave when only his head and my pack were left above the surface, but he was making it.

'*Kohat*. Strong,' Superman muttered, somewhat grudgingly.

Yunis certainly was strong. I doubted that I could have even lifted my rucksack over my head, let alone stay upright with it in that water.

'He'll have to come back,' said Bruce, wearily. 'I can't do that with mine.'

He wouldn't have to. At the far bank Yunis walked back

upstream to a point opposite us, dropped the rucksack and launched himself back into the river. I filmed him making another crossing with Bruce's pack, then took the camera across by the same method in order to film Bruce bringing across the black box. Five hours later we crawled out of the final section and up on to the west bank, hardly able to speak.

Trekking northwards once more, Bruce and I discussed the apparent weakening of our bodies. We didn't need his expertise in the field of sports nutrition and fitness to know that we were eating far less than we required to carry heavy loads through this terrain and maintain good health. Yunis had gone on ahead with Superman, dropping back only once to make a clumsy attempt at stealing my *parang*. Just when he must have thought he had been successful I retraced my footsteps and picked it up from under the tree where he had stashed it for collection on his return. We could hardly wait to get to Meruli's little trading-post.

The next day, when we reached it, Meruli was in his usual position, squatting by the door, chain-smoking self-rolled cigarettes and scrutinising lumps of *gaharu*. He had convinced himself that a ghastly accident had befallen us and was thrilled to see us, full of questions as to why we had taken nine days and not five. He had to wait. We had fallen upon the 'cold cereal' bag like pirates around a treasure chest. It took the edge off our hunger while a vast rice and vegetable chilli dish was prepared. I ate such a huge amount that I spent the remainder of the day in agony.

PART II

11 PORTER TROUBLE

25 January

We ate a lot today, 'cold cereal' snacks, 'four seasons casserole' with rice, tinned sardines with rice, and a chicken. I am still hungry. Perhaps my stomach is taking no chances after the last nine days and is still sending panic signals to my brain. I certainly haven't done anything physical to work off each successive meal. I've just been writing an *aide-mémoire* of the last two months. The rain that has pounded on Meruli's roof of rusting steel and tattered plastic without let up since last night has extinguished all hope of Yakop pursuing me across the Eilanden with my diary. It's a shame, but the thought of him using it to light his fire is more amusing today than it was yesterday. In the meantime it's been fantastic to take the weight off my right foot and keep it dry. It's healing fast, as are Bruce's, but we have a new problem.

When last here in Sera Dala our discussions with the locals gave us no cause for concern over the question of porters for our hike into the mountains. Everyone has agreed that 35,000 rupees per day plus food, is attractive but as yet we have no definite sign-ups and it's not looking good. We want to leave tomorrow for Lukun, the first of three villages that apparently lie in the foothills to the north. Perhaps later tonight, during the usual gathering around Meruli's oil lamps, some men will come forward.

26 January

Our friends in Jakarta insisted that our chief problem on this trip would revolve around porters. Bruce and I paid little heed to this, confident that our own easy-going and friendly, modern approach would succeed where others had failed. How naïve. As I returned from a river wash this morning I saw Bruce sitting amid twenty or so men in the middle of the airstrip. Superman informed me that they had wanted to speak to Bruce alone, confirming our suspicions that his Indonesian face and superior manner have not been helping in these matters. I didn't interfere but filmed the event from various angles with the mountains glowering in the background. Bruce returned, downhearted, with the news that no-one would come with us as a porter, or even as a guide. No reason was given. The money on offer was still good. Bruce had even offered to get rid of Superman if it would make a difference. They just did not want to be our porters, and now only one option remained. Leaving all but the essentials with Meruli we would have to go to Lukun, two days away, and try to find porters there to return with Superman and collect our food. It was, and still is, a gamble, not least because we might not find our way there without help. The little village of Lukun is not marked on any map and all we have to go on is the instruction: 'Follow the big river north.'

The path has become increasingly difficult throughout the day as the valley leads us ever further into the foothills. Wherever the river has cut itself a sheer sided gorge between towering spurs, we have been forced to climb up these and then down the other side. It is a tortuous routine of gain and loss, and so steep that for once I'm glad of the web of tree roots criss-crossing the path. Without the hand and footholds they provide our frequent falls would be messy. We are no longer walking but mountaineering. Ligaments and tendons are tensioned like hawsers and on the few stretches of flat ground, at the top or back down at the river, feel as if they have been overstretched and no longer fit.

At five o'clock we were still on very high, steep ground. To camp we needed water, and a flat spot large enough for Bruce's bivi-bag, so decided to attempt the next descent and reach the river hopefully before dusk. It began to rain with tropical ferocity and was cold, so cold that when we reached the bottom I opted to switch from hammock to bivi-bag as well. The only apparent spot big enough for both of us was a dank space beneath the barbed leaves of a big *rattan*. Superman's hammock was ten metres away. With darkness upon us and no let up in the downpour hammering on the sheet over our heads, we cooked with my steel mug on its little stand over a lump of hexamine fuel rather than fiddle around with matches and saturated wood. It was a miserable spot and there was enough time only for one serving of casserole shared among three because the river was rising with startling speed. A huge pile of boulders that just half an hour before had stood two metres proud of the greenish water was now invisible. As the water lapped ever closer it seemed wise to find a safer sleeping site.

Bruce is now on the slope above me somewhere, and both he and Superman have declined further food in favour of the warmth of their sleeping bags. I am actually enjoying myself. Having cleared a reasonable spot and stretched a sheet over it, I made one last foray out into the deafening darkness, first to find Bruce and get the camera, then to Superman for another helping of powdered casserole. I did ask them if they would like me to bring them some hot food in bed. Their refusals saved me the trouble. Having changed into dry clothes, I filmed myself sitting on my pack and cooking a generous mugful.

28 January

There is still no sign of Lukun but at least we now know we are on the right track. At around one o'clock we met a group of women from the village on their way to Sera Dala. With flouncing dirty skirts and strong feet they came bounding down the streambed above us until our greeting stopped them short. They balanced on a boulder as they bent forward to peer down through the overhanging branches. We shook their hands at the top of a small waterfall and they beamed back at us, the two younger ones wide-eyed and coy behind the matriarchs. One thrust forward the naked toddler she was carrying on her shoulders for a good look at us and they all shrieked with laughter. This was the first time we had met such a group without their men in protective attendance, and here, perhaps, was a hint as to why: the younger women flirted with us unashamedly. Bruce asked how far remained before Lukun and was told it was an hour uphill and another one downhill.

At this point a burst of whooping calls announced the arrival of the missing escort – they had gone off after a pigeon. They leaped from rock to rock with astounding speed and agility, carrying only their bows and arrows. With a better command of Indonesian, the men had a different version of the route ahead. They advised us to look for the cave in the next valley and stay there overnight.

Despite the solitary feeble stalactite hanging from the middle it is not quite a cave, but more one of those precarious overhanging boulders the size of a house that will one day just topple. With ample space, wood and a big pool in the river for a bath, it makes a great camp. Last night in the rain and mud was fun in its own memorable way but I love nights in the jungle when I have the time and resources to be well-organised, well-fed, dried out and comfortable.

29 January
More a bouldering exercise than a trek, the trail today was mostly along the river, over piles of enormous rocks worn smooth and slick with frictionless algae. It was excellent climbing practice but slow work. At one point, where the path climbed into the precariously clinging forest to skirt around another impenetrable gorge I was faced with the most impressively dangerous section we had yet come across. The path stopped at a sheer rockface of dripping limestone. It took me a few moments to realise I hadn't taken a wrong turn and that the path continued on the other side. It took longer still to spot what I was supposed to hang on to and stand on in order to get across. There was no ledge. Looking down there was only a fatal drop to the river crashing far below. It didn't require more than five complete moves, but for three metres only a few sketchy-looking finger and toe-holds kept

me in defiance of gravity. Looking back at Bruce coming across I reflected that, under normal circumstances, without a rope I would most likely have shied from such a risk even without a heavy pack on my back.

With another ridgeline still in front of us it was clear that we would fall short of Lukun tonight. At a spot where two rivers of equal size joined, we found a flat spot big enough for one bivi-bag. Soaking cloud moved silently through sullen greenery that hung heavily in a matted state of waterlogged decay. I scoured the rocks for almost an hour to find a pathetic bundle of fuel but the wood up here has a core of spongy pith that will not ignite. Eventually we achieved casserole-boiling-point, and the fire died.

At this altitude (1,700 metres), with every stitch of dry clothing on, my Gore-Tex jacket laid over the top, and wet clothes on top of that, I wake up frozen to the bone. I'm going to have to ask Superman to give back my sleeping bag.

30 January

I can scarcely believe that it is taking us so long to reach this damn village. If, and it is if, we make it tomorrow, it will have taken us six days. That we are slower than the locals is understandable, but three times slower than them is demoralising.

This morning the most beautiful sight enriched a drab awakening. A small boulder was covered on one side with butterflies, wings open and slowly flapping. There are over ten thousand species of butterfly in New Guinea and this one rock sparkled turquoise, silver and red.

The path, once we had found it, climbed steadily to new heights and into a moss forest: every tree, stick, stone, root and fallen log was covered with a thick, glistening carpet of every hue between dark green and earth brown. The coating is so thick over everything that the path through the trees is often reduced to a narrow tunnel and arches through which we crawl, dragging our packs behind us. The lowland forest has a sort of 'sameness' about its predictable shapes and heavy colouring but up here the trees are twisted and gnarled into fantastic forms, interweaving into a vast sculpture, free of sharp edge and abrupt angle. It looks strangely alive, like a scene from J.R.R. Tolkein's *Middle Earth*, and just as treacherous. Sometimes a hand flung out to grab a tree, plunges straight through the spongy-sheath of moss to find a useless honeycomb of rotten wood behind. Sometimes it appears that we are walking well above the ground, across a latticework trap of elevated roots hidden beneath the moss. Bruce likens the experience to laying rotten carpet over the top of a rusty, children's climbing-frame then walking along it blindfolded.

We were all caught out this morning when the river disappeared. We didn't notice at first, so intent were we on skirting the huge boulders and washed down trees that cluttered the narrow ravine then I became aware of the unusual silence. The river was buried beneath what must have been an ancient landslide and the path was leaving it for another detour into the clouds. We should have gone back to fill our water-bottles but expected to find a stream soon enough. It was five hours before we did so, by which time I had become desperate enough during the relentless climb to squeeze out handfuls of moss just to wet my mouth.

31 January
At long last we have made it and I am filled with a deep respect for the people here: man, woman, woman-with-child, they routinely make that journey in two days, against our six. Small in stature they nevertheless possess a strength, stamina and agility that would, perhaps, put even world-class athletes to shame. And looking around Lukun it is not hard to see why. From the moment the young children are capable of clambering through the high doorways of their families' beehive huts they spend their entire lives either climbing or descending a steep slope. Between one hut and the next is a steep slope. The paths fanning out to their crops are, in places, almost vertical. Despite haphazard terracing, their fields are so steep that they hardly need to bend over to dig up the vegetables. The river far below the village is a continuous grade four or five rapid all the way. Going to the

loo involves negotiating a one in four gradient mudslide that has already terrorised Bruce and me - it ends with a sharp drop into the pit. The only two level spots of any size are home to the church-cum-school and a helicopter landing-pad that has been painstakingly carved from the ridge. Apparently a missionary supervised its construction but it has never been used.

There were times this morning when I would have appreciated being winched up into a helicopter and flown the rest of the way. We knew we would make it today but the path just kept going up and up. Every time a descent offered hope we would find ourselves climbing once more, regaining the height we had just lost. Occasional gaps in the trees offered glimpses across the valleys, but never enough to see the lie of the land in front or to tell where Lukun might be. The map was of little use, for while we could plot our course with the GPS across its longitude and latitude grid, the ground surrounding us rarely matched the contour lines around each carefully pencilled cross.

Finally, the rate of descent began to exceed that of ascent, the moss gave way and we stepped out on to an almost clear felled spur of sun warmed fragrant ferns. Roughly hewn planks lay stacked against a tree and the path became a red earth highway spotted with the imprints of countless human toes. Unmistakable this time, voices drifted up the convex slope and on another spur to our left there were patches of terracing adjoining solitary *pondoks*, tiny in the distance. Superman vanished ahead, even keener to arrive than Bruce and I.

Further down still, a platform of grass afforded a stupendous view across a junction of four valleys and the precipitous cloud-topped hills between them. It took me a few seconds to notice the knot of round roofs several hundred metres below us.

Superman must have been there for at least ten minutes already, because a man and a small boy were coming up the slope fast. They shouted excitedly when they saw us and came on even faster. There was barely time for introductions before they were tugging at our packs, insisting that we hand them over.

'We've taken six days. Allow us this last remnant of dignity, please.' I spoke firmly in English, refusing to let go. Ibrahim, as the boy introduced himself, made a grab for the camera box instead and set off happily after Bruce who had neatly sidestepped our other assailant. The man, wouldn't respond to anything I said in Indonesian and continued to paw at my rucksack until I set off down the hill. It was one of the most frustrating slopes yet encountered, horribly steep but with no roots and branches to help me control my knees. Mud and loose stones combined with a surging desire to get there set off a series of tumbling falls that triggered each time a chorus of '*Awas, awas, awas!*' Look out! The damn village never seemed to get any closer and my last few steps into it were the stumbling, uncontrolled run of a delirious desert traveller towards a mirage.

The entire populace, it seemed, was lined up in two ranks to greet us and we shook hands with everyone. Beneath the eaves of the nearest hut two, gnarled, old men waited silently for us to reach the end of the line. They alone were unclothed, sporting boar's tusks through their noses, rattan waistbands and spectacular penis gourds. They looked like ancient warriors, the last of their kind, armed now with a century of stories, faces impassive but eyes shining with pleasure at the reverence we showed them. Essou the man in whose spare hut we were staying, told us later that we should address each as *Bapa Tua*, literally meaning 'Old Man'. '*Bapa Tua satu*, one, *Bapa Tua dua*, two' he said.

1 February

Our first day in Lukun has been a rest day, principally for Superman who, understandably, did not want to set off immediately. It was also a day for consolidating the porter situation and buying the food that will fuel their four-day journey over the route we have just taken, then back again with the rest of our kit. They are led by a beaming, tightly wound bundle of muscle called Nehemia who burst from the torrential rain into our hut last night, scattering children and assuming instant control. I liked him immediately: he has tremendous enthusiasm and energy and is clearly a leader here. He seems inseparable from the other man who came in with him last night, Yunam, the only man going back to Sera Dala who adheres to the traditional dress code of penis gourd and nothing else. These men are tough: in discussion with Yunam last night I wore three layers of clothing while he sat there in nothing but a dried vegetable.

The deal we thrashed out is that they will get R20,000 each per day (£2), plus R5,000 per day for food. If they make it back in four days they get a bonus day's pay. We have split the load seven ways to speed their progress. If, after that, they can take us further up the valley our problems will be over.

We still have to discover where they intend to take us though. Lukun is nowhere near the original route we intended to follow, yet Nehemia insists he can have us at the foot of Mandala in a week. From our current position on the various maps, we cannot see how and suspect they are confusing Mandala with Puncak Yamin (4,581 metres). As we pore over the maps it is with the knowledge that any firm planning is useless until we know the route to the next villages, Bebecleh and Krabu. All we know at the moment is that the route begins through the valley opposite us. From here, however, we can already see that this valley has two branches between almost sheer sides, each of which corresponds with the map, and the villagers all give different opinions on which of these we must follow. In *I came from the Stone Age,* Heinrich Harrer wrote of his Papuan (Dani tribe) porters and the sense of resignation that came to him with the knowledge that they, not he, were leading the expedition. That is probably the case with the Una people here. We'll just have to wait and see which mountain they're planning to take us to. We've learnt enough of the unpredictability of porters in Irian Jaya not to attempt to forge our own route and expect them to follow. It would take too long in any case and involve too much food and money. However, if they get us to the foot of either mountain and can then be persuaded to ferry our food to a decent altitude we may find ourselves within striking distance of both the summit and our trek out to the north.

Unusually, the sun stayed with us today until the chilling

shadow filling the valleys below us had crept up the slopes to Lukun's eyrie-like position. In those last minutes I filmed a closing chat between Bruce and Superman. There is little point in his returning to us here once he and the team have reached Sera Dala so this is the last evening with our friend, and I am sorry to see him go. We've had a good laugh together. He would be an excellent guide to the more Indonesian parts of Indonesia, but here he has had a more difficult role - that of employee and close companion amid what is to him a foreign land.

12 THE UNA TRIBE

2 February

Our visas and travel permits expire today, but how little meaning those bits of paper seem to have in this place, among a people who until recently had been unaware of international borders and political demarcation lines. I feel a million miles away from the nearest man to whom a rubber stamp and desk are axe and hoe. The only aspect of our new status that is of the slightest interest is that we will henceforth be accumulating, at £12 each per day, a hefty bill to get out of Indonesia, which has serious implications for our budget. But we are going to climb the mountain.

Just after first light this morning Superman and the Magnificent Seven departed, Superman not feeling too well. He has the first symptoms of malaria so I have lent him my spare shirt for the journey. If it is malaria then he should have a good forty-eight hours between this attack and the next, by which time he will be in Sera Dala. Nehemia is carrying his bag.

For Bruce and me it has been a day of eating and equipment repairs. The cameras needed cleaning and drying out having suffered their first real dose of saturating humidity. The main camera broke down yesterday, helpfully flashing an easily recognisable drop-of-water symbol in the viewfinder to tell us why before we fished out the screwdrivers and had a go at it. We dared not dismantle too much but fortunately a few hours of sunlight with the cassette door open seems to have done the trick. It's those bits of equipment that have constantly borne the brunt of the damp and our incessant falls that are really showing the strain. Trousers are ripped, and our boots already look as if they have covered thousands of miles. Bruce's much-prized rucksack, supposedly indestructible, needed heavy duty stitching.

Mine is a disaster area.

It is cold and foggy outside. Darkness and cloud descend together on this place. Wood smoke rises from the conical roofs to fill in any gaps so that navigating the slippery paths by torchlight becomes like walking through smog. After such a long journey from Sera Dala our candle supply is down to one small stub and my torch batteries emit a dull beam only after I have warmed them in my pocket. Only those huts with a fire have any light so we are forced to go to bed as soon as supper is over. Through our window, contrasting against the chilly draught, I can see chinks of firelight among the houses cluttering the slope below us. I wish we were in one of them.

3 February

Our stay here has become one long challenge as to how best to fill the time between meals. It is extraordinary how the body reacts to periods of food rationing, such as on the six-day journey here. Now that there is food a-plenty we can't seem to get enough. No sooner than I have polished off an enormous plateful than I am ravenous once more.

I spent a creative hour scouring the village for 'establishing shots'. A flower here, a woman making a basket there, a man picking lice from his son's hair, a view across the roofs to the bananas hanging from a tree beyond. Even a hen with her chicks did not escape the lens, but more interesting footage came from a vast colony of cyrtophora spiders stretched between two large bushes on the edge of the helicopter-landing pad. Viewed from beneath, this silken patchwork of individual orbs was all but invisible against the clouds so that the hundreds of spindly occupants appeared to be floating in mid air, unsupported. I hung around for the first big catch – a praying mantis. It was ensnared then engulfed in a communal feast.

I've been surprised by how seemingly at ease the villagers are in front of the camera. Only some of the young teenage girls dart away, giggling, and that is clearly more to do with having our attention on them than apprehension before the lens. The boys all leap into the frame, destroying the spontaneity of the shot, while the men appear indifferent. The women smile coyly then avert their eyes. Very small children burst into tears. Essou tells us that, apart from missionaries, no Westerner has ever stayed in Lukun.

They want for little here. Bananas – sweet ones, perhaps the most delicious I have ever eaten - are abundant and they have papaya, too. Three different types of potato grow alongside taro on crude terraces. Spinach and cucumbers are supplemented by other vegetables which I couldn't recognise from the shoots. After the monotony of the powdery *sago* and indigestible, baked, green bananas of the Korowai region, spinach and potato are gastronomic heaven.

With so much time on my hands I have found myself thinking more and more about my relationship with Bruce. Although we have hardly exchanged an angry word on the whole journey that doesn't mean that we do not get annoyed with each other. The most contentious aspect of the journey is the camera work. It is not that we disagree with what should be filmed or how to go about it, there's something else – an atmosphere between us when the camera is out of its box.

There are also differences in our views on trekking. It's important to Bruce that he carries all he possibly can and that the expedition is as 'hard-core' as possible. After all – he's an ex-Marine. For me the trip is hard-core as it is and, more than anything, I want to enjoy it. I hate carrying heavy weights: the couple of quid a day for an extra porter to lighten our loads would be money well spent. I'd feel more like filming and would take in more of my surroundings. I might even notice some of the wildlife that's supposed to be here. Tree Kangeroos, bandicoots and dozens of other massupials abound in the forests. You would think that the three-metre-long emerald tree monitor and the iridescent breastplate of the riflebird would be easy to spot, but I have seen little more than a cassowary's footprint and the huge grasshoppers we have eaten.

4 February

This afternoon Bruce and I confronted each other in front of the lens. So far we have not revealed our gripes and grievances to the camera and were in two minds as to how to go about it - in front of each other, or alone with the camera. Since we are getting along well we decided to film each other. It should have been daunting but we were in high spirits setting it up.

I don't think I said anything to surprise Bruce but he certainly had one in store for me. Apparently, ever since a remark I made in jest when we were drunk at a party in London, Bruce has been worried that my intention was to portray him in a bad light in front of the camera. I was appalled to hear this, and even more so to hear that certain events and remarks I have made during the expedition have reinforced his anxiety. It was all I could do to hold the camera steady as he spoke. I had been, he said, reluctant to be filmed when tired or limping yet keen to film his own injuries.

'Bruce, how could you think that?'

'Well, what was I supposed to think?'

'I was drunk, for God's sake!'

We ended up laughing and it was if a cloud had lifted. I could sense enormous relief in Bruce. I don't think he had really believed it of me, but the nagging doubt had been there and there's nothing like the monotony of trekking to turn a nagging doubt into a deep-rooted suspicion.

The villagers will sell us their stone axes for as little as R5000 rupiah (fifty pence) each, so tomorrow we will invest. *Bapa Tua 2* wants me to buy his and although it's not the best on offer I'll take it because he's an old warrior. The axes seem inferior in comparison to the Dani tribe ones I saw hanging on a wall in Jakarta, and selling for vast amounts of money in Bali, but I would rather have one of these any day. The axes made by the Dani in the Baliem valley have beautifully-worked and polished heads of dark green stone set in sturdy handles. The Una axes consist of crudely-knapped shale lashed to little more than a forked stick. Technically, they aren't even axes – the Una blades are set perpendicular to the handles, making them adzes, not that the distinction matters here. To my mind, however, the main difference between the two is that those of the Dani are made for the tourist trade while those of the Una are proper tools. The Dani have been using steel for over fifty years and probably sold the last working stone axe decades ago. Any axe I buy here in Lukun will have been used that day by a man who possesses no steel. I don't care how chipped the blade is, how grimy the handle, or how ill chosen the stick, for my axe will be the real thing.

5 February

Boredom has set in. We have just finished another delicious lunch, and I am plagued by hunger. Essou and his wife, Ayrsenna have been neglecting the banana situation so there's nothing to snack on. A child at the door is gnawing a baked potato and I am dangerously close to mugging him. Our meals are the daily event here. Each mouthful is relished and the last is anticipated with dismay. Four hours until the next!

Bruce has started a course of antibiotics. While the various wounds and ulcers on my legs, arms and hands are showing signs of improvement in the drier conditions, his are still a mess and producing vile quantities of pus. There will be no respite for them once we move off again and with so many to tend he is at some risk of septicaemia.

We have filmed about all we want to of Lukun. This morning we were invited to enter the *rumah laki-laki*, men's hut, for the first time. There aren't many men around at the moment but the two *Bapa Tuas* with their nosepieces and penis gourds are by far the more colourful anyway. *Bapa Tua 1* donned a cassowary feather headdress and sang for us in a quiet but strong voice. He's a bit of a character. Later when he appeared, armed with bow and arrows, his chest and face painted red with the dye extracted from *bua mera* seeds, it wasn't difficult to persuade him to put on a hunting act for us. Through the long grass behind the *rumah laki-laki*, with great stealth and cunning, he stalked a cucumber laid on the bank before us, loosing off an arrow straight to its middle.

It was little more than tongue in cheek filming, but we had to do several takes before the children around us had been persuaded to keep quiet and the hunter himself had stopped cackling.

Less than twenty years ago this village was at virtual war with the next, Bebecleh, and while all are friends now, the old man carries the scars of axe and arrow wounds from those times.

6 February

It's Sunday so we went to church. Where the Asmat were Catholic and the Korowai weren't interested, the Una are Protestant. According to Matthius, the preacher here, a Dutch missionary converted Lukun to Christianity along with the other villages in the area in the early 1970s.

In the church about two-thirds of the village were sitting on the floor with the women on the left facing the lectern, and the men on the right facing every direction. The *Bapa Tuas,* against the wall at the back, were asleep before the service started. It seemed a pleasantly informal affair – one or two men were even smoking – but once the service was under way the blank expressions on most faces couldn't be mistaken for anything but boredom. For most of the time Matthius spoke in the vernacular but the readings from the New Testament were given in Indonesian, a language that few here speak. Only the women seemed to put any effort into the two hymns, and various small children howled throughout.

'Not much difference, then.' Bruce remarked dryly as we stepped back into the sunshine afterwards. 'Not that I go to church often, but the crap singing and people dozing off was quite like an military service, don't you think?'

7 February

Our porters returned last night amid heavy rain and the grey light of a misty dusk. Nehemia exploded through the door again, scattering children. We were glad to have them and our kit back but my sleeping bag was missing. When Superman had departed with symptoms of malaria I had a feeling that things would go wrong with our agreement that I should have it back for the mountain. I could have insisted that he left it and my spare long sleeved shirt but he was ill. Apparently he had had to be carried for much of the second day and I know how awful a high fever can feel - the all-pervading chills accompanied by profuse sweating. But when he decided to hang on to the sleeping bag he was in the warmth of Sera Dala.

Wrapped in a bivi-bag each night for the last week, I have been wearing all my clothes and yet still wake at around four shivering with cold. Bruce, on the other hand, climbs into his sleeping bag naked and reports having to undo it each night to avoid sweating. I think he quite enjoyed telling me that. I'm a touch worried at having put myself in this position. If even half our plans go ahead, Bruce and I will be sleeping above four thousand metres for some time, double the height we are here. I'd love to be able to look forward to long nights of comfort and warmth, but I'll have to resign myself to snatching moments of sleep between bouts of shivering. Essou has a blanket and might sell it to me. If not, one consolation is that the adventurers of old had to make do with so much less.

The *rumah laki-laki* was rocking tonight. Everyone who went to Sera Dala was in there and the *Bapa Tuas* were on top form. To huge applause they and their shadows danced around the walls in a re-enactment of the battles with Bebecleh in which they took part as young men. Each holding an arrow to his bow, they darted through the flickering light as if running among the enemy's huts, whooping wheezily and twanging their bowstrings at the invisible foe, the split bamboo floor bouncing and creaking with every footfall. *Bapa Tua 1's* eyes shone in the firelight as he sat down, the rest of us shuffling around cross-legged to make room for him at the hearth. His tall friend, he said, had once carried him back from Bebecleh after he had been wounded. He owed his life to his friend, he said, and now they were the last of their kind in Lukun.

13 LED ASTRAY

8 February

In a touching display of goodwill and hospitality, almost the entire population of Lukun gathered at the edge of the spur to say goodbye as we shouldered packs and gingerly picked our way down to them past the men's hut. Once again we made a point of shaking everyone's hand. *Bapa Tua 1* seemed particularly sad to see us go and held my hand in a strong grip for some time. The years had dulled neither his curiosity nor his humour and I felt certain that behind his leathery face lay the kind of wisdom that transcends the perceived complications of life in our century and cuts straight to the core of human spirituality. One might have thought that if any of these villagers were to resent our presence and the march of change it represented, it would have been this old man and his comrade-in-arms. Instead, I could not escape the impression that he felt honoured by our visit. I hoped that my respect for him had not gone undetected.

There was a moment of confusion when we picked up our loads again: a large slice of the crowd also swung up their string bags and adjusted the straps over their foreheads.

'How many people did we hire?' I asked Bruce. He looked helplessly at me. In addition to the six porters on the payroll we now appeared to have three extra men, Ayrsenna, and three children - thirteen in all.

Despite the mud I was determined to disappear from the village with sure-footed dignity and marched boldly over the lip of the landing pad, aware that *Bapa Tua 2* had somehow got in front of me and was already disappearing among the bushes below, a new stone axe slung over his shoulder. Ramming my heels into the earth for some semblance of grip I heard the first chorus of

'*Awas! Awas!*' as Bruce went down heavily somewhere behind me. I felt pleasingly strong, determined to show that my pack was not a problem, and glad that I was out in front and that my falls were out of sight of those following. Above me I detected growing annoyance in Bruce's voice at each '*Awas! Awas!*'. He was now being forcibly helped down the path.

When I reached the river *Bapa Tua 2* was nowhere to be seen. I stumbled through the shallows, feet sliding among the slimy rocks, and was almost on to the makeshift bridge when a chorus of horrified shouts from behind stopped me. Nehemia's hands signalled that the bridge would not hold my weight.

'Come back! ' Bruce shouted, above the rushing water. 'They want to carry our packs!'

At almost any other point in our journey since Mabul, I would have welcomed such a suggestion, but now I replied with genuine indignation. 'No way!'

As Bruce explained to them that we were content to take it slowly, I watched their faces. They were genuinely anxious, afraid even, for our safety. Essou was pleading.

We set off again with our loads, upstream and past the bridge.

Just round the corner the men were already manning a more solid looking bridge. Four slender poles lay wedged between boulders, spanning only the middle, unwadeable section of the torrent. As we approached, Nehemia and Yunam had already finished lashing an additional support spar to the flimsy looking handrail and now stood chest-deep in the racing water at either end of the bridge, ready to hold our feet in place on the greasy wood. Humbly, we passed from the grip of one to the other before splashing over to the far bank to watch everyone else scamper across nonchalantly. We, two, hardened explorers glanced at each other helplessly.

In the hours that followed, however, I came to understand the villagers' concerns. If our route to Lukun had thrown challenges before us, it had nothing on this path. It was clearly less travelled and the reason for this became clear when we crested the first spur high above the river and Lukun. In the far distance our companions pointed out the village of Langda, its airstrip just visible above some low cloud drifting through the valleys. For the villagers of Bebecleh this would be their trading-post rather than Sera Dala. They wouldn't want to negotiate the longer path to Sera Dala unless it was absolutely necessary.

After that first climb we traversed a grassy slope, keeping parallel with the edge of the precipice that dropped two thousand feet to the river below, angling the edges of our boots into the narrow ledge left by passing feet, testing each hold, one step at a time.

Suddenly I found myself dropping. The path beneath my left boot had offered only the briefest resistance before it gave way. The tuft of grass in my right hand tore free from the earth as I twisted myself into the slope, scrabbling for a hold with my left, the immediate surge of adrenaline all but drowning the screams of '*Awas! Awas!*' The edge of the precipice was less than twenty feet away and I was sliding towards it. My left hand locked on to another tuft but it pulled free almost immediately. I flung out the same hand again to grab at a tiny shrub but it was too far away. Panic surged through me. My hands were now locked into claws, raking the slope, fingernails ploughing through the wet grass. My leg muscles were forcing the inside edges of my boots into the ground, searching for friction, or the smallest lump that might stop my slide towards the edge. Suddenly my right boot hit something and I speared my right fingertips into the slope, then grabbed a prominent tuft with the left. The downward slide stopped. For a few seconds I lay there, moulding myself flat to the ground. I dared not move a muscle. I just lay there, looking along my left arm at the pathetic tuft of grass in my hand. Its roots were visible, all but pulled free of the earth, and I knew my boot was against nothing bigger.

'Mark! Mark!' The shouts of my companions drifted to me as the panic subsided. My head was only some five feet below the path but I knew without looking that my boots were less than ten feet from the edge of the cliff. I turned my head to look upwards and

I saw Yunam crouched low into the remains of the path, reaching down for my right hand. Nehemia's fingertips were stretched out inches from the left. He adjusted his position and made contact, hooking his fingertips around mine. I knew I wasn't helping but I dared not move as I was inched back to safety.

'Jesus Christ, that felt close.' Was all I could stammer.

The main problem with the trail was that no foothold had ever previously experienced a hundred kilos of weight. The local men, usually only tipping the scales at around seventy with their loads, could step confidently with an experienced eye, but under Bruce or me the same piece of ground was liable to give way without warning. As we continued along the path I felt at a further disadvantage in being behind Bruce and offering the *coup de grace* to ground already strained by him.

Up and down, over and under, the path wound along the side of the gorge until we dropped into a smaller ravine entering from the right. Here, another river emerged, then crashed over the lip of a deep waterfall. The water seemed in slow motion as it plummeted through the air.

I turned my attention to the bridge. It ran right along the very edge of the drop, just two feet above the water hurtling into space. And it wasn't a bridge, just a bundle of loosely bound saplings, green with algae and wedged between rocks. Yunam and Essou both gripped my arm and pointed to its flimsy poles. '*Awas!*' they implored.

I heard Bruce giggle in front of me. 'Don't laugh, Parry. It's your turn for a fall!' I told him. Bruce had not had a decent mishap all day.

Nehemia crossed first to drop his load beyond the narrow ledge in the rockface opposite, then returned to offer a helping hand off the bridge. Bruce was next, crossing without a hitch and depositing his pack out of sight round the corner. He returned with the camera.

The three poles underfoot were slippery but felt solid enough, and in no time my outstretched right hand was in Nehemia's grasp. Then, without warning, the pole under my right foot snapped and

I pitched backwards, my foot plunging into the water, my fingers wrenched from Nehemia's. I tried to grab hold of the little man but my hand slid off his elbow and flailed in space. My left foot slid along the remaining poles and lodged against the rockface. My right hand slapped on to the stone, searching for something to hang on to. Time had slowed down. I had to find a hold. My hand settled on a tiny ledge below Nehemia's feet, and searched for grip at its edge. As my weight yanked at the tendons supporting my hooked fingers I was dimly aware of a searing pain shooting up my forearm but my grip held and I swung into the rock, my fall stopped. Hanging on grimly, suspended between my left hand and foot on the remaining poles and my right hand on the rock, I could feel the water tugging at the bottom of my pack. I wasn't aware of Yunam leaping to my rescue through the water, or three others jumping on to the remains of the bridge. While Bruce filmed and everyone else shouted advice in one of Irian Jaya's 255 languages, I was aware of only one thing: the water tugging at the back of my pack. If I allowed either of my arms to straighten and the pack to lower, the current would flip me upside down, under the bridge, and into one of those rare videos that capture someone's death. I concentrated on trying to find something beneath the water to put my dangling foot on.

For a second I felt vaguely in control. Nehemia now had my right hand and was pulling with extraordinary strength. I could feel someone else trying to lift my rucksack from behind. It was going to be all right.

A loud crack resonated through my head as the rest of the bridge snapped and Nehemia gave a cry of alarm as my weight almost pulled him in on top of me but his grip on my hand did not slacken. I watched the broken ends of the poles scraping the rock. Then they snagged on a root and people suddenly surrounded me, all trying to heave me up the rock. One of the porters, Pyet, was downstream of me and the bridge, standing on something below the lip of the waterfall, the water crashing against his waist. I felt hands all over me pushing and pulling and inch by inch I was propelled to safety.

Bruce was still filming. 'Say something mate!'

Only one word sprang to mind but it wasn't very camera friendly.

'Well that's the second time in half an hour when I felt I was going.' I managed a smile and looked away, down to the water falling into the gorge below.

While the last of the team waded across we went ahead to a patch of sunlight to film my trembling knees and shock. Little segments of the drama came back to me as we walked and I remembered Pyet's expression as he stood beneath me. His eyes had shown no fear, yet if the wood had moved again he would have had little hope. I felt humbled by his bravery and selflessness.

Concern still showed on the faces of our companions when they caught up with us, but disappeared as I attempted to thank them saving my life. '*Saya belum matti! Terima kasih banyak*! I am not dead yet. Thank you very much.' My Indonesian was not up to emotional outpourings but they got the idea and laughed.

An hour later we arrived on a narrow outcrop at the foot of a sheer rockface against which lay a ladder. A collection of poles had been lashed together and now stood in a loose scaffold against the twenty-foot face. Above them I could see a decent-sized ledge, then another scaffold running up the second face. Apart from the bark lashings there didn't appear to be anything to stand on but for the occasional stub where a branch had been hacked off. I could see what was coming and prepared to capitulate without a fight. Essou and Matthius moved swiftly to stand between us and the ladder, and the others crowded around until everyone was packed on to the tiny bulge. As Bruce began to argue I dropped my pack, almost knocking Ayrsenna off the edge and poking my eye out on the end of Yunam's bow. There was a brief moment where everyone seemed to be holding on to everyone else. Ayrsenna brushed aside my apology but glanced at the ladder, then at me, imploringly. She needn't have worried: I had not the slightest intention of going up it with a pack on. Bruce hauled himself up to the first stub but it snapped off immediately and he slid back down. The argument was over.

That old feeling of weary resignation returned as I watched the first two shin up the poles with our packs swinging from their shoulders, strong toes finding grip on the tiniest lumps in the wood. Essou and Matthius added to their own loads those of the first two men and followed, to an accompaniment of whooping calls from Nehemia. Then there was a sudden rush to get on to the ladder, as if no one wanted to be in the way when Bruce and I fell off it. We nearly went over the side anyway as everyone jostled for position, leaving only Nehemia and Oskar, our oldest porter, on the outcrop with us. As they climbed they all joined in with the whooping song; it sounded as though a flock of bizarre birds were calling to each other. Coming from a land of written and orchestrated music I found their sounds beautiful, a song without rules or boundaries. Perhaps it is the only language common to the many different peoples of Irian Jaya. Yunis, our guide out of the Korowai area, had made similar sounds at every river crossing, and so had Mr Homburg as he paddled us down the rapids of the Eilanden river. Back then I thought it sounded like a prayer to the spirits in the face of something hazardous, but now it seemed more like a celebration of life's excitements.

At the top everyone had gone, our packs too. There was nothing we could do about it, and I set off with a spring in my step. Bruce was furious: he would no longer be able to say that he had carried his share all the way. But it wasn't long before he, too, was appreciating the joy of walking through such a stunning and impressive landscape without having to stare fixedly at the ground ahead.

For several hours we were on a well-defined stony path that snaked its way round a mountainside that could have been in the Alps or the Rockies. Small scrubby bushes and tufts of grass clung to the rocks on either side; and the air had that piercing purity only found above massed vegetation. After weeks in mud and forest it was clean, refreshing and beautiful so we took our time.

Soon enough the first drops of rain were falling and another ladder took us back down into the mud and clinging trees. We were losing the light and Nehemia, repeatedly darting ahead then stopping to wait, was impatient for more speed. As I crossed a small obstacle he relieved me of the camera box and then made off. Bruce likes to find and stick to his own pace and would not be hurried, preferring to come in last with Oskar, whose countenance implied that he, too, would not be hurried. For me that last hour was a race, though I doubt Nehemia ever felt his lead threatened. Every time I felt in a position to elbow him out of the way and storm past, my flailing feet would catch on a root or a stone, sending me face first into the dirt. When we reached a deforested and partially cultivated spur I knew I was on the home straight and redoubled my efforts, determined not to be beaten to the top by a five-foot-tall man carrying almost twenty kilos of food, the camera box and his bow and arrows. With rain and mud streaming down my face I gave that slope everything I had left, clawing at the grass on all fours across the steeper sections, sprinting between the terraced fields of potatoes, puffing and grimacing like a weightlifter. Nehemia simply ran up the spur. He never slowed down. I watched him disappear into the cloud above as my feet shot from under me again and I fell on to my hands and knees, spent.

9 February

A good night's sleep, it seems, is rarely experienced by the people living in the mountains of Irian Jaya. In Lukun I had assumed that if they were hardy enough to run around in the frequently chilly air at 2000 metres wearing at most a T-shirt and shorts, then the nights spent by a small fire would not pose a problem. Last night in Bebecleh, however, Bruce and I were billeted in the men's hut and fresh evidence on the matter was presented. The circular hut bulged with around thirty people, of all ages from teenage boys to the three wizened old men sitting silent and almost invisible in the gloom. The focal point was the square hearth in the centre of the floor and the mood within the hut mirrored the condition of the fire. As the light outside faded, the wood was piled on. The flames threw warm light out to the walls as everyone vied for the best position in which to dry themselves, and the day's events were noisily debated. At each of the four sides a strangely ordered shuffle of positions relative to the fire continued without interruption to the chatter; those wettest and coldest first, until everyone had had their share and the atmosphere was as thick with steam as it was with smoke. It was rather like being in the midst of a colony of Emperor penguins weathering the Antarctic winter, the circle constantly moving so that each had a go in the sheltered middle. Feeling the goose-pimples disappear from my arms and watching the steam rise from my clothes I sucked in the heat until another took my place, pushing me a step closer towards a spell on the outside where the cold air, in this case coming through the loosely bound slatted walls, would suck it away again.

As the flames died and the embers were arranged for cooking, the conversation dwindled. Phase two of the evening had now begun. String bags were emptied, the potatoes and taro buried in the glowing mound, and everyone settled down to wait, content to listen to the inevitable few who never stopped talking. The cold crept back into the centre of the throng. When the last of the food had been withdrawn from the fire, wrenched into pieces and passed round, more wood was stacked on for phase three. Fuelled now by food, as well as a second dose of warmth and light, the mood in the hut became more animated and lively. But eventually, one by one, each man made his space and lay down to sleep on the bamboo slats of the raised floor through which, the cold air whistled. Feet towards the fire, arranged like the spokes of a wheel but without the gaps. And that, I thought, from within my blanket, would be it for the night. I hadn't reckoned on phases four, five, six, seven.

I was woken by a hubbub of low voices and creaking floor to find that everyone was up and once more pressing in upon the hearth where a new fire was being built. It wasn't even ten o'clock and they were all freezing. When the fire died again so they all went back to sleep, until the cold woke them, and the pattern was repeated all night.

I felt annoyed at being constantly woken. Surely, in all those thousands of years, they could have come up with something, to ease the passage through the long nights. At the very least they could tighten up the walls or devise something to sleep on. The lowland Asmat had comfortable, draught-proof mats for this purpose.

A hand nudged me awake. Cooking had been going on and I could smell a freshly-baked potato. It had been left on the edge of my mat. I was dimly aware that it was in danger of rolling away so manoeuvred an arm out from under my blanket. Too late - off it went. Oskar grabbed it, gave it a vigorous slapping, to remove any new dirt, and handed it back.

'*Terima kasih banyak.*' Thank you very much Oskar. '*Selamat pagi.*' Good morning.

'*Selamat pagi!*' chorused the dozen or so men squatting round the fire.

I sat up and watched the men, shoulder to shoulder in front of me, a wall of backs. I could tell from the movement of the shoulders who was stoking the fire, splitting a potato, passing a piece, turning over a drying leaf of tobacco, or holding up an ember to light another's cigarette. There is an informality and intimacy about proceedings here that only exists in the Third World. It's sad how much in the West has been formalised: in every aspect of daily routine we are kept apart from our fellow human beings somehow and even from our own family. Privacy, hygiene, economy of effort, comfort and personal space are all great concepts, walls, cookers, tables and prams all welcome innovations, but there's nothing to suggest they've been of fundamental benefit to anyone at a spiritual level. Then again, abject poverty can hardly be recommended. The Una people are probably among the last on Earth to be 'well off': they want for little, yet remain virtually uninfected by materialism. They are just too remote up here for it to be either available or in their faces, and it's hard to think of any innovation – apart from blankets – that would make a great deal of difference to life on these slopes.

Bruce is ill again. His system normally produces vast amounts of wind, but something about our current diet is not allowing him to get rid of it. In the mornings he moves slowly and painfully, is distracted and uncommunicative. Everyone knows how unpleasant and debilitating trapped wind can be but I have to assume the problem lies deeper. He is almost at the end of the course of antibiotics and the sores on his legs and hands appear to be clearing up. It doesn't therefore seem to be septicaemia. Bruce is one of those people who are never ill without good reason and I think that his body is fighting off something more serious than indigestion. As usual he apologises for being dull company but my concerns lie only with the mountain ahead: we can't expect an easy time of it and he will need his strength.

Just before we left Bebecleh I was reminded of another possible cause for his malaise when I saw him taking his weekly anti-malarial tablet. The side effects of Larium are well publicised and principally psychological but everyone reacts differently. Bruce has taken it before, on a project in Sumatra, but stopped when he found himself becoming excessively irritated by the expedition nurse. On the path to the next village this morning he was in a weird mood and it was impossible to tell whether it was due to his illness, Larium, or both. I sensed that he didn't want to talk so walked along in silence, listening to him cursing Nehemia under his breath. Eventually, he begged me to come past and take his position behind our talkative guide, who could not be discouraged from offering a helping hand over every obstacle. I underwent the remainder of the morning being yanked off-balance to the accompaniment of 'Awas!' and laughter from Bruce. I ended up laughing too. It was impossible to be angry with Nehemia: he was determined to help and would brook no opposition, least of all from whoever was clearly in need.

Every cloud has a silver lining, and Bruce's weird mood was perhaps largely responsible for a massive uplift in our fortunes when we reached the next village just before lunch. It was called Aliryi. Nobody had ever mentioned a village called Aliryi. Nehemia now informed us that the next village was called Kap

Kap. We looked at the villages on the list I had bought from Sera Dala.

'What happened to Krabu?' snapped Bruce, as we sat down on our packs in the middle of a crowd of excited villagers. 'I'm not moving another foot until we've sorted out exactly where this picnic outing is taking us!'

'Good morning!' a voice interrupted, in well-pronounced English.

'What?' We both looked up at a well-built young man who had elbowed his way through the crowd and now stood over us.

As a young boy, Sibet had been chosen by the village elders of Aliryi to go all the way to Wamena for his education. He had already exhausted his supply of English, but had a look of measured calm that set him apart from the wide-eyed mob jumping up and down to get a better look at us. Immediately he grasped our lack of grip on the language and spoke in slow, measured tones. Even better than this, he pointed in the right direction when we hit him with the usual first question: 'Where is Mandala?'

'How do we get there?' I asked, and he motioned that we all sit down again.

'Have you a pen and paper? I will draw you a map. I have been there.' Bruce and I looked at each other in disbelief.

Within fifteen minutes we had a route drawn out noting village names, and how long it would take to walk to each. Mandala was almost two weeks away but there was a path from here. There was no path to anywhere from Kap Kap - Nehemia had indeed been leading us to Puncak Yamin. A broad smile enveloped Sibet's face as the two of us rattled through the new plan. He knew what was coming. 'Yes,' he answered, 'and my friends will help carry your bags.'

The crowd had dispersed, distracted by the arrival of two enormous clusters of pandanus nuts (known locally as *win*) that Yunam and another man else were hacking open with their stone axes beneath the door of the nearest hut. I scanned the scene for Nehemia and found him watching the three us with what might have been a wry smile. It broadened at my gaze and then he vanished behind some women holding tiny children at their breasts; he disappeared at the most extraordinary angle, as if he had dived headfirst into the *win meleé*. I was still pondering this unusual exit when he suddenly appeared in front of me, beside Sibet, and thrust a clump of nuts into our hands.

'Nehemia!' Bruce's voice had a ring of playful admonishment. 'You take us to the wrong mountain! That's Puncak Yamin!' He flung out an arm over Sibet's shoulder towards the darkened massif that, so late in the afternoon ended abruptly in a horizontal shroud of cloud. 'Still twelve days walking to Mandala!'

Nehemia laughed and shrugged apologetically, slapping Sibet powerfully across the shoulders. 'Bruce, Mark, Sibet will be a good guide for you now.'

I breathed a sigh of relief and searched his eyes for disappointment or bitterness. There was none. I would have found any animosity created by this change of events hard to bear. We owed so much to Nehemia and the others from Lukun, my life for a start.

There were still the others to tell but Bruce was on his feet and managing, in his own inimitable style, to make a joke out of the situation, playfully shaking Nehemia by the shoulders all the while. The whole village was in an uproar of laughter. The furore took some time to subside and by then our other porters had decided among themselves to bail out. A further two weeks' walk was not for them. They wanted to get back to Bebecleh by nightfall so wasted no time in collecting their things. After an emotional farewell they departed.

My gut instinct tells me that at last we have ironed out our problems with guides and porters. Sibet will do his job well and may even fill the role of third cameraman, a post left vacant since Superman's departure. His friends are all young, strong and eager, and sit around me now noisily discussing what they will do with their impending wealth. We represent the first employment ever to hit this village and are hiring extra men to lighten our own loads and get to the mountain in a time near Sibet's estimate. I'm in high spirits tonight.

The only negative aspect of the evening emerges from my reassessment of our finances in the light of such a long march yet to go. The totals at the foot of the notebook make depressing reading, just like my bank statements. We've known for some time that crossing the island is beyond our resources but now we're forced to admit that even making it into that magical area of 'Relief Data Incomplete', north of the mountain range, is unlikely. We both wanted so much to finish with a stint of high adventure and desperate endurance but can't afford it. It's all taking too long, and the amount due to Indonesia's immigration authorities is growing. The decision we have both been avoiding, to finish on the mountain, was finally made when Sibet told us that the tribes further north were no longer traditional.

While I struggled to find a way out through the figures, Bruce sat in deep contemplation of the ration logbook. Suddenly he gave a shout of triumph. He had worked out that we could now afford to resume eating our dried food. At a reduced rate of two mugfuls a day we would have enough left to climb the mountain. I wasn't so sure: common sense told me that if we ate it now we might end up heaving a bag of potatoes up Mandala because of some unforeseen delay in getting there. Bruce ranted on about protein deficiency for a full five minutes, then threw in the decider: he was sure that a daily dose of our own food would cure his debilitating stomach troubles. I capitulated and we had a mugful of cereal to celebrate.

14 BACK ON TRACK

10 February

We have landed on our feet with these boys. They tear around in front of us, hacking a veritable motorway through the forest, erecting handrails, renewing rotten bridges and cutting footholds into the endless fallen trees from which we would otherwise plummet. It took no time at all for them to realise the full extent of our ponderous lack of agility, and also that we do not want to hear '*Awas! Awas!*' when it's already too late and we are in mid-air. The cries continue but with a note of friendly mockery followed by peals of laughter when we hit the dirt.

For some reason we have eight rather than the agreed seven, so Sibet has taken a cut in his extra wages as head porter, guide and cameraman to finance the last member of what is clearly an inseparable group of friends. More than anything we want a happy team and if that means bringing along an extra then so be it. I am just getting to grips with their names: Sibet, Kremos, Bliss, Menias, Niram, Well, Touson and Tremas.

It was more than a day's walk to the first village so we stopped after only six hours at the only *pondok* on the way. Perched on a mossy arête and taking up the only piece of flat ground for miles, it was just big enough for the ten of us to squeeze cross-legged around the fire. Later Bruce and I felt our way out to the tiny door, through the blinding smoke billowing from the huge pile of damp wood Kremos was still piling up, and set about trying to find somewhere to put a hammock and bivi-bag so that the others would have more room in which to spread out and sleep. From outside, through streaming eyes, the little *pondok* looked as if its walls and roof had caught fire. Smoke spewed through the roof thatch and from every crack. We tried to visualise arrangements amid the thick undergrowth that dropped sharply away on three sides.

Suddenly the entire team charged out after us, snatched my *parang* and leapt into the foliage. The thwack of steel biting into green wood drifted up the slope and into the cloud obscuring the tops of the trees. Not more firewood, surely?

I'd failed to realise the full worth of our new team. Within ten minutes a framework platform had broadened the top of the arête to a width great enough for a bivi-bag and baggage storage area and Bruce was stringing his hammock between two firmly-braced uprights. Earth and moss went over the platform, followed by armfuls of ferns, and, bingo! I had the springiest mattress since the Sheraton Hotel in Timika. The basha sheet was strung over the top just as the inevitable afternoon deluge started. They were delighted at our enthusiasm for this new and most pleasing of developments and eagerly tried out the completed arrangements themselves. Menias ventured that my bivi-bag was of just the right proportions to get really cosy with a girl and I was left marvelling at how the expression 'jiggyjiggy' has somehow conquered the world.

11 February

The weather held fair for much of the long walk to the village of Dirik. At the top of the day's first hill, a rocky knoll above a moss forest, dotted with miniature bushes not dissimilar to heather, Sibet had a go at his new role of cameraman. He grasped quite quickly the basic functions and framing of the subject with the smaller second camera but we could not get him to hold it vertical. Every shot looked as if it had been taken on a tripod with one leg shorter than the others. It was as if a life spent largely in a place with no flat level ground and a jagged horizon had left him incapable of recognising a horizontal plane. Time and practice would solve the problem, we thought, and now that we were no longer planning to cross the island there was less pressure to conserve cassettes. We handed over the camera and told him to shoot us whenever he felt like it. If we were to get just ten minutes of decent footage out of the next few weeks it would be worth it.

After miles of heavy rain and thick mud we slid into the village of Dirik looking as if we had been at a rainy Glastonbury festival. We couldn't go into someone's home like that so set about wiping off the worst with handfuls of grass to the amusement of a dozen faces peering out of little doorways. Eventually two young women scuttled through the rain with pots of water that they tipped down our legs, pointing out the bits we had missed with hoots of merriment.

14 February

It has taken another three days to reach Sumtamun, the next village, but they've been easy ones. Informed by Sibet that just four hours lay between Dirik and the first of two *pondoks,* we made the best use of the glorious sunshine that by seven o'clock was purging the village of the night's rain. The solar panels were put on full productivity amid a jumble of drying clothes, boots and basha sheets. We sat on our packs waiting for the beeps that indicated a battery was fully-charged, and dressing sores that covered our legs, arms and hands. I noted with alarm that several of mine were very deep. Fringed by bright red swelling they were about the size of the Ngorongoro crater and probably had just as rich a variety of animal life hanging around within.

When we reached the *pondok* it had been raining for several hours. Bruce set up the camera to film the process of arranging sleeping quarters, but it was a disaster. When we had finished he found that so much water had got past the protective cover that the camera had switched itself off and the viewfinder was full. Carefully, by the light of fire and candle, I removed as many tiny screws and bits of casing as I dared and we took it in turns to hold the sodden camera next to the fire. We hardly spoke for worry that it would never work again. If we are to tell this story in film there remains so much vital footage yet to take. Gunung Mandala was the first aim of the expedition and, as we draw closer, the mysterious south face, the 'stupendous abyss', exerts an almost magnetic grip on me. It frightens me too - so unknown, so remote, so unlike anything I have attempted before. Do we have enough equipment to climb it safely? Will I have the courage to take a few risks if we do not?

When the others showed signs of wanting to bed down for the night we reassembled the camera and tentatively flicked the switch. The familiar whirring noise and glow from the viewfinder spoke the good news. 'Thank God for the Japanese! I'm going to bed,' said Bruce.

When I woke in the morning my boots, dried above the fire overnight, were outside the door of my bivi-bag. This was good. It was more like the expeditions of old, when porters did not go on strike or steal your kit, but made the journey easier.

It was an auspicious start to a day in which our enthusiastic team scored high marks for effort, field skills, cookery and hospitality.

We had been given to expect a long, hard day, and being enveloped in drizzly cloud without break did little to alleviate the grind of a tortuously steep uphill slog. But once again Sibet had underestimated our speed and when we finally broke out of the moss forest to climb the last few hundred metres to the top of a 2,813 metres peak over which, the path meandered, we were two hours ahead of schedule. The next *pondok* lay just half an hour's descent away and the majority of the porters ran ahead to start work on a fire. We took a breather and watched Kremos stalk a *merpati*, Irian Jaya's answer to the pigeon. As we dropped our packs he sprinted off, stringing an arrow to his bow as he ran. I wished I could follow and film but knew it would scatter his chances of success. My boots and light coloured clothing were no match for his all but naked stealth. Against the fire-scorched slope, probably lit by a lightning strike, his dark skin would be virtually invisible to the bird looking down. The *merpati's* only chances lay in him missing or snapping a twig underfoot. The little bird was clearly aware that something was not quite right, but had not made up its mind as Kremos closed on a good firing position and drew back the four-pronged arrow to full stretch. Thwack! The bird tumbled through the branches, the four-foot arrow lodged in its breast. A hoot of triumph drifted up the slope.

Looking eastwards from this vantage-point I could see a major junction of two valleys in the distance. One could be followed almost from the foot of the hill we were now on, straight and deep, broadening out in the middle then closing up again to form an impressive eastern entrance. Through those 'gateposts' I could see the other, running from south to north like the main road of a stupendous T-junction. It looked much bigger and deeper, the eastern wall almost black under the cloud shrouding its top. Could this be the valley by which we had originally intended to approach Mandala? I got out the map and compass while Bruce confirmed our latitude and longitude with the GPS. It was. We had come almost full-circle. The last two villages on Sibet's list would lie along its side, and not much further north Mandala's lowest and most south-westerly spurs would plunge into the valley floor. With a shock I suddenly realised we should be able to see the summit from here and looked up from the map. Of course it was in cloud, but its sudden nearness startled me.

As we pushed through the branches overgrowing the last few yards before the hut, we could hear feverish activity. What hut? Only a broken and rotten frame remained. Naturally, the others were not the slightest bit put out and had already collected most of the materials required for its rebuilding: poles for the framework, broad leaves for the roof, and bushy branches for the walls. Even before we had the camera set up the old skeleton had been cast aside and a new one was taking shape, practised-hands lashing together the cut and trimmed poles with strips of bark. I couldn't see the whole process taking longer than forty minutes. I thought back to the jungle training I had done in the Army and remembered the shambolic shelters we had all erected, then watched fall down again. These lads were good.

An hour later, squeezing as close to the fire as possible, I sensed that something was afoot. The boys kept patting their stomachs and laughing. Surely that little *merpati* was not the reason for so much gastronomic excitement. Bruce noted my puzzlement. 'Have a look over there.' I followed his finger.

In the corner, arranged upon a platter of broad leaves, lay the *merpati*, alongside a frog and a furry creature the size of a cat.

'Oh, no!'

'I think it's a *cuscus*, quite a sweet looking little creature. Here, have a look.' He passed it over.

In my relatively extensive experience of eating local delicacies in far-flung lands, the appearance of an animal prior to cooking had little to do with its effect on me. The meat might be delicious, but as guest of honour you are often more likely to be presented with an eyeball or the left ventricle. I'm a touch squeamish and prefer not to have a mouthful of fat, gristle, or the various bits of anatomy that rarely, if ever, get as far as a butcher's shop. Insects don't do it for me either. Watching the *cuscus* having its luxuriant fur burnt off I thought longingly of the pasta Milanese in the bag I was sitting on.

When the moment came, however I was passed a kidney and a chunk of roasted hind leg – delicious. Next came the frog, cooked in a leafy parcel among the embers. No problem there - it was so tiny that, split ten ways in the smoky gloom there was no way of knowing which bit I had been given anyway.

'*Enak!*' Delicious! We heaped compliments on the chefs as we waited for the main event. I followed the procedure closely:

Merpati Mange-tout

1. Take one pigeon, plucked and cleaned, and dismember it. Place half the pieces centrally in a star-shaped arrangement of large leaves.

2. Cut the white heart of a palm into thick slices then place half of these on the pigeon bits.

3. Preheat at least four fist-sized stones in the fire and remove quickly when the first has exploded. Put out any fresh fires that have started.

4. Arrange the hot stones on top of the chopped palm-heart then cover them with the remaining palm heart and then the remaining pigeon bits.

*5.Close up the leaves into a parcel, pinning it tight shut with wood
splinters.*
6.Place on the fire and weight down with large flaming logs.
7.Wait twenty minutes. Treat burns with cold water.
8.Serve with a sprinkling of salt.

We were each given a whole breast (they would take no refusal)
and it was one of the most tender, mouth-wateringly delicious
pieces of meat I have ever tasted. The palm-heart tasted of
little more than water but, with a bit of salt, made the perfect
accompaniment. The bird was a touch on the small side, so out
came the potatoes and we thought that was that. Without us
noticing, however, they had cooked up one last leafy bundle and
now presented it with the flourish of a magician pulling a white
rabbit from a hat. In it was a huge pile of the chanterelle-like
fungus I had seen growing from the trunks of trees, steamed to
perfection by another hot stone. Served on leaf plates it exhausted
my stock of superlatives.

Well spaced out over a relatively gentle slope, Sumtamun, the
village we have now reached, is more of a town. Interspersed
with the traditional round huts there are houses built of wood and
concrete, with tin roofs and glass windows. A noisy classroom
fell silent as we walked past and on to a large flat area marked
out as a sports pitch. Further on a white hosepipe ran on stilts
from a central tap to a grove of trees a little higher on the hillside
where the smartest home looked over the village and down to the
airstrip running parallel with the river below us.

'*Camat?*' I asked Sibet warily, indicating the house on the
hill.

'Doctor,' he replied. He pointed out some other buildings of
note. 'Kiosk, MAF radio, *rumah laki-laki.*' We had arrived at the
men's hut.

The two incumbents, from an outlying village, greeted the
invasion of their peace and quiet with stoicism.

'Right!' Bruce had a look of steely determination about him.
' I'm feeling thin. I need to do some carbo-loading before this

mountain. I'm off to the kiosk and there'd better be some Super Mi there or there'll be trouble. If I eat one more potato....' He trailed off. 'Are you coming?'

'I'll just fish out a fresh wad of cash. I take it we'll be emptying him of stock?' But he was off to the kiosk and its promise of a meal of biblical proportions. Super Mi (super noodles) was the only potato-substitute for miles. Ever since Sibet had mentioned there was an airstrip at Sumtamun Bruce had been seeing the little packets dancing provocatively before his eyes. If this shop had none, the village's chicken population was in for a heavy and sustained battering.

The shop was empty but for a box of pens, a few bars of soap and a carton of forty Super Mi with seven more packets lying loose on top. 'Chicken flavour!' Bruce was clutching his prize.

I paid, having added two bars of soap as the porters had requested. Within an hour we had demolished ten packets of Super Mi between us and lay on the grass outside our hut, unable to move, oblivious to the crowd of onlookers. They could never before have witnessed such a display of gluttony, but I had begun to realise how thin I was becoming. Every muscle was visible under the tightly stretched skin and they all looked really small.

15 Febraury

First job of the morning was to pay a visit to the Missionary Aviation Fellowship office where a man sitting amid a dozen car batteries was listening to a jumble of radio calls between what sounded like every airstrip in Irian Jaya and the MAF headquarters in Wamena. We asked what chance there was of getting out on a Cessna in three weeks' time.

'You want helicopter!' It was a statement of fact rather than a question.

'No thanks. A Cessna is good.'

'No! Helicopter is good! *Wakka-wakka-wakka-wakka-wakka!*' His arms flailed about his head, eyes bulging.

'Helicopter much money.'

'Arrggh! You are *bulay!* No problem!'

'Cessna money no problem. Helicopter money big problem.'

'Arrggh!' He made no effort to hide his disappointment. We would have to go and see the doctor, he said. The Doctor had also asked for a plane around that time.

The MAF will fly light aircraft and helicopters on demand, but like to have as many seats and as much cargo space paid for as possible. They would be unlikely to send an aircraft just for us unless we paid extra. We went to see the doctor, a frail-looking Indonesian who appeared and sounded in need of medical attention himself. His home was well-furnished and clean, had wooden floors and comfortable chairs. The floor to ceiling bookcases were packed with medical volumes titled in English. In broken English he told us that he was indeed in need of medical attention but was hoping to combine it with some sort of doctors' meeting in early March. We chatted for a while but he looked impatient for us to leave, so we did. I suspected he would have gone by the time we returned, but for the moment our departure was set for 6th March, exactly three weeks away.

The radioman took the news well. *'Cessna, Cessna, tidak masalah*. No problem. *Wakka-wakka-wakka-wakka-wakka haha-haha!'* His crazy laugh followed us outside.

With that sorted, there was just one thing still to do before we headed on towards the village of Tabasik. We needed to have a long chat with the porters about Mandala.

Ever since Aliryi neither Bruce nor I had mentioned climbing the mountain. We had not known how many local authority figures might crop up before we got there and did not have much confidence in the ability of people in these parts to keep a secret. As we had drawn nearer to our goal, however, Sibet had revealed that the elders of the last two villages, Tabasik and Biblangda, would not allow us any further. We had not asked whether this was through concern for our safety or for political reasons but our failure to confront this news had led the boys to believe we no longer wished to climb it. Now they were talking about turning round before the base of the mountain.

As the evening wore on our local audience departed to their

huts. Bruce revealed the true plan: we were going up Mandala, no matter what, and alone. Protest filled the little hut. Their concern for our safety was not just touching: given the constant sight of us stumbling and falling along their village paths it was understandable. But they knew nothing about rock climbing, had never seen ice, let alone touched it. Tents and clothes were the main issue, though: the porters would have no materials to build a hut and would freeze. To counter any argument to the contrary we described the cold, and other aspects of mountaineering, in the most dramatic terms, standing over the fire, casting wild shadows over the walls, re-enacting past experiences and fibbing horribly.

'*Mandala kecil! Gunung di Nepal besar - es semua, dingin sekali! Tidak pondok engkau matti*! Mandala is small. The mountains in Nepal are big - all ice, very cold. Without a hut you are dead!'

Then we brought out our trump card: Bruce's crampons. It was highly unlikely that we would use them but their fears for our safety fell away. In a thousand years they could not have envisaged such an extraordinary piece of equipment. One by one they strapped them to their bare feet in reverent awe. Even our amazing camera, the very latest from Japan, had not elicited such a response. The argument was won. They would help us to establish a base camp at the tree-line before they returned. In the meantime they would not mention our plan to anyone until we had broached the subject with the *kepala desa* of either Tabasik or Biblangda. And we have several cards to play in persuading him to let us go ahead. One, in the best traditions of artful cunning, is to throw a big party. Since we were back in the Asmat region we have been planning to hold a feast near the end of the journey, to celebrate a great trip and express our gratitude collectively to the people of Irian Jaya. With the money for the pig already aside, it's really just a question of where. Sibet gave us the answer: Tabasik, he informed us, was the only village with a view of Mandala.

A colourful lively spectacle in the shadow of the mountain - it sounds perfect, and not least for the camera, which has yet to witness a ritual or festival. Birth, marriage, funeral, harvest festival, eating an enemy, adolescence to manhood, exorcism: not one party has crossed our path. Christmas Day in Agats didn't really count. We don't want to stage-manage some obsolete ritual but hope that if we put up the food and the justification, the people will guide the rest.

16 February

The porters know nothing of the covert planning behind the forthcoming party, of course, but the idea put paid to any lingering disappointment from last night. The sun was out today and spirits were high. At the last river before Tabasik they dropped their loads, stripped naked and leapt into the water brandishing their new bars of soap. Was this for the party or was Tabasik renowned for its abundance of pretty girls, I wondered.

'Just the party, I think,' said Bruce, an hour later, as he scanned the village belles.

Later, as we spun the tale of our journey so far to the *kepala desa*, a carefully-spoken man in his early forties dressed smartly in trousers and a polo shirt. Danger signals flashed when we were asked our opinion on the Indonesian annexation of Irian Jaya, but until our true goal was revealed we were in easy territory. Every time the boys interjected in the Una tongue we listened carefully for the word 'Mandala' but they seemed to be keeping to our agreement. Like the one other Westerner who, long ago, according to the chief, had ventured this far, we had come only to look at the mountain.

As Bruce gained support for the party I looked around at the village. Straddling a saddle between the main slope above and a wooded hillock marking the point at which the spur continues its plunge to the valley floor, it commands unhindered survey of two valleys. We have just left one. The other is the same we would have walked along over a month ago if all had gone to plan. Scattered banana palms swaying in the breeze break up a view that promises to be magnificent in the cloud-free morning air.

I was longing to see the mountain and this evening escaped the noisy racket of the men's hut to find the whole massif silhouetted against the light of a million stars. Just an immense black wall, miles long and thousands of metres above me, outlined against the sky. I called Bruce outside to watch the moon rise from behind it, and briefly he forgot the stabbing pains that had returned to his stomach. He whistled quietly through his teeth at the sight.

'*Abom!*' The loud, throaty cry startled us. One of the two impossibly old *Bapa-tuas* had crept up behind me and now gripped my arm. '*Abom!*'

'*Bahasa Una*. Una language.' I turned to find Sibet perching in the high doorway of the men's hut. 'Gunung Mandala *nama Abom.*'

'Well, that's what we'll call it from now on. It's their mountain,' said Bruce. 'That sort of thing might help our cause with the *kepala desa*. Sorry, I've got to lie down again.' He tottered off, leaving me in the grip of the old man. We chatted for a while.

'*Abom!*'

'*Abom!*'

Then, he yanked hard on my arm and began to act out what he wanted to say. I got it in one. When he was a child, and right through to his becoming an old man, *Abom* had had a headdress, a hat, all year round. Now there was no headdress.

Global warming: Mandala's icecap has melted. It's not entirely unexpected. The glaciers on Puncak Jaya, have receded to half their length since it was first climbed in the fifties, and our friends in Jakarta said there had been little left on Mandala when it was climbed for the second time five years ago. That said, in his 1993 study of the ecology and vegetation of Mount Trikora, New Guinea's second highest peak, Jean-Marie Mangen noted that Mandala was still covered by 'eternal snow'. We had hoped there might be something left. I congratulated myself on having left my crampons behind in Jakarta but still feel robbed. How ridiculous that all our research in London had never turned up this fact. Perhaps the only people besides these villagers who knew were the pilots who fly over it on their way to isolated little grass strips in the middle of nowhere.

15 PARTY TIME

17 February

The day of the great party dawned bright and clear. The immense black wall of the previous evening was now a limestone cliff, still too far away for detail, its crest running almost flat for several miles from the summit area in the north-east towards the rising sun, then dipping behind the intervening hills. The Mandala massif is essentially a huge slab of ancient sea bed that has been thrust skywards at an angle, like a badly laid paving-stone sunken on one side but elevated on the other. I was looking at the 'stupendous abyss' we had come so far to climb. Behind that solid barrier of cliff-face was just a gentle incline down towards the northern jungle and another fifty miles of foothills, the route of the two previous climbing teams. As the south face was as yet untouched by the sun and partially hidden by the curve of the valley, I could only make out the top of the first spur climbing from the river to the base of the thousand foot cliffs, like a gigantic supporting buttress to the wall above. It was a fantastic backdrop for the festivities.

There was a definite buzz in the air as I agreed a price for the medium-sized pig tethered to a stick at the grassy entrance to the village, and made a large donation towards whatever else was needed. In the middle of the village an enormous fire was already burning, heating the rocks that would do the cooking. There was only one thing left for me to do, and I wasn't looking forward to it.

Peals of laughter were coming from inside the men's hut where I knew Sibet and the others were dressing for the occasion. As I wandered over, Bruce's head appeared in the doorway. He was laughing. 'Get over here, Anstice. Your penis gourd's ready.'

A cheer went up as I climbed through the little entrance. I was confronted by a scene straight from the changing rooms behind an international fashion show. Several men from the village and all our porters were in there, trying on feather headdresses, poking boars' tusks through the holes in their septums, plaiting rattan round their waists and generally preening themselves. It was all good kit for wooing the girls. Bruce and I had an assortment of dusty, second-hand penis gourds to choose from.

The laughter that accompanied our 'fitting' brought such a crowd of faces to the door that some of the warriors had to chase their owners away, and stand guard. Getting into mine was the least comfortable experience I had had since the bridge had snapped beneath me. Bruce couldn't find one that fitted until our hosts, after a search among the houses of the village, triumphantly produced something that appeared to have been used as a tobacco pouch. It was repulsive, more like some prehistoric prophylactic than the fine-looking long and pointed ones the rest of us wore, but he loved it.

Outside, the village women waited. All were dressed in grass mini skirts, or *salis,* and sporting necklaces of seeds. One or two also wore bird-of-paradise feather plumes, but the majority were bareheaded or had wrapped strips of colourful netting round their hair.

'Keep everyone here for a minute. I'll go outside first and film you all coming out,' I volunteered courageously, then stepped smartly outside into the sunlight and screams of laughter from the assembled women and children. The hilarity died to an appreciative murmur as, one by one, the splendid-looking warriors climbed out, all muscle and feathers, then rose to a fresh crescendo when the last man appeared. Did *I* look like that? The grinning apparition performed a proud pirouette, skinny white backside and legs covered in sores with a shiny black vegetable in front. Holding the camera steady was difficult.

I escaped to film the unfortunate pig being led to its demise. Whatever sacrifice I felt I had made for this event it was nothing to the ordeal this animal was about to undergo. Without preamble,

Sibet fired an arrow from point blank range into its heart as it struggled against its tether. We waited for the squealing to stop, and a well-practised routine began.

The leaves and branches sealing in the heat of the fire were removed and the pig's bristles burnt off in the flames. On one side of the men's hut, the women had already lined a pit, three feet across and eighteen inches deep, with banana leaves and had a big pile of vegetables ready. The first layer of hot stones was removed from the fire with wooden tongs and arranged on the leaves around the bottom of the pit. A layer of vegetables followed, then another layer of leaves, then more stones, and so on. The pig, now cut into joints went in last, in layers. Then the base leaves were curled around the whole pile and weighted in place with the remaining hot stones.

While the feast cooked the *kepala desa* led a short, open-air church service but everyone was fidgeting and it didn't last long. When the last word had left his lips the men grabbed their bows and arrows and formed a large circle on the only piece of flat ground in the village. The women followed, spreading out around the edge. 'This looks promising.' Bruce muttered.

Sibet told me later that it was a dance traditionally performed at the advent of battle, but if I had been an enemy spy lying in the long grass above the village and looking down I wouldn't have been overly alarmed. The men shuffled around in single file figures-of-eight and opposing concentric circles, with regular stops during which Sibet would lead a song. It spoke to me more of 'Ooh, I hope we don't get hurt!' than 'Let's kill them all and steal their women!' Perhaps it had been toned down and rechoreographed by the missionaries. Or perhaps I was missing the point. Nevertheless it was an engaging and colourful display and some of the women accompanied the action with fantastic warbling cries.

At the end of the dance we asked the men to demonstrate how, in the good old days, their war party might have attacked another village. I wanted to feel a shiver of fear as they sprang out of the long grass and rushed screaming towards and over me, but they hopped about randomly, twanging their bowstrings and bumping into each other.

Soon a delicious smell was filling the village. As everyone dropped their weapons and ran to the leafy oven I was left wondering whether the Una really had ever had such a warlike past as we had imagined. Even on the way to church, the Asmat canoe warriors would have been sure to put on a convincing and bloodcurdling display if asked, or paid, to do so. There was something about the Asmatters, besides their recent history, that left me in no doubt of their capacity for violence. Whether it was the heavy brows over faintly bloodshot eyes, or the sinewy muscles on all but the very oldest men, or the feeling of 'gang' that surrounded the longhouses and their drumming ceremonies, it never took much imagination to visualise a sudden attack and my brains being sucked out through a straw.

The Korowai had not seemed overtly dangerous. They were willowy figures, in small groups, flitting through the trees, yet it was precisely that ability to come and go so noiselessly and suddenly that highlighted our vulnerability. Their potential for violence was in their unpredictability and their distance from Bruce and me as citizens of the Earth. We were trespassers on their turf and knew nothing about them, except that they were armed, and accountable to no law that we knew.

The Una are just too nice. They're happy and smily and put up with too much noise from their children. They go to church and have fallen over each other to help Bruce and me. Perhaps their new religion is the key. They are Protestant while the Asmat are Catholic. The Catholic missionaries had a laissez-faire approach while the Protestants, by all accounts, would have forced these hill people to burn every symbol of their ungodly past, don clothes and cease revering the old heroes and legends. Bloodshed and warfare perhaps now seem no more than a joke to the peaceful and charitable inhabitants of Tabasik.

But, then, perhaps not. The peaceful scene around the lunch preparations was fast disintegrating into a brawl. As I was focusing the camera on the opening of the oven I was elbowed aside by at least two people and an extraordinary feeding frenzy erupted around me. The village had split into its family groups. As they sat apart from each other in little circles around banana leaf platters they seemed to dispatch their most aggressive members into the mêlée to capture as much of the spoils as possible. The cooking pit was buried under a shouting mass: small boys crawled out between men's legs clutching a taro or a fistful of spinach, then dashed to their families to drop it off before they hurled themselves back in. If the piles of food within each family circle were anything to go by - no one family appeared to be doing any better than the rest - there must have been some element of order and control behind the riot, but I couldn't see it.

By the time I got close to the pit the last scraps were being cleared out and the dogs were moving in. 'Are we going to get any do you think?' I sat down despondently on the grass beside Bruce.

'Doesn't look like it. Here, have a smoke instead - it's about all I can handle at the moment anyway.'

Before I had a chance to feel aggrieved Menias and Bliss brought over two lumps of meat, choice bits, of course, and some spinach. The pork was tender and succulent.

Before everyone dispersed we dished out the last of the beads, pencil-sharpeners, razor blades, folding scissors and pocket-knives. Now that *Abom* was our final goal we would no longer need them. One of the knives, a cheap and nasty switchblade, no more than a gimmick in the West but an impressive gadget out here, we presented to the *kepala desa* as a final bribe towards the coming negotiations.

18 February

Knife or no knife, this morning went swiftly wrong. We were procrastinating over the right moment to come clean. Nothing had yet been said and we were sorting out the day's loads in the open. I was wondering why we were still paying for eight porters when we now had so much less to carry. Perhaps the *kepala desa* saw one of the ropes or the boys, talking among themselves,

155

had let something slip. Whatever, he was suddenly accusatory and a man I hadn't seen before was furiously pacing up and down before us and the gathering crowd, shouting indignantly, stamping his feet and waving his arms in angry gestures.

'Who the hell's that?'

'I don't know. He's not very happy is he.'

Sibet filled us in. He was the *kepala desa* of Biblangda, the next village. Absentmindedly toying with his new flick-knife, Tabasik's *kepala desa* told us quietly that we would have to pay R5 million (£500) to climb the mountain. Click. Out came the blade again. We looked shocked, then forlorn.

'I'm sorry, but we do not have any more money.' Barring that set aside for our porters and flights out, it was no lie. Click. The chrome-plated point sprang from its handle.

As this information was relayed to the shouting man, we conferred.

'How about telling them we've already paid a million in Jakarta?' I suggested, eager to be of some help to Bruce, who looked desperately tired and as if he would rather be anywhere else. It was not an outright lie for we had indeed paid to come to Irian Jaya: it was just that our travel permits said nothing about this area, let alone going up Mandala.

Bruce translated the plan.

Both *kepala desas* were now on their feet and shouting, not so much at us, I was reassured to note, than to the villagers who now stood around in a big circle.

'Sibet, what are they saying?'

'They say it was wrong of you to pay someone else to climb their mountain. The *kepala desa* wants you to go back. He will not let you climb *Abom*.'

I felt a fool. We hadn't wanted to drag politics into this but I had done so unwittingly. As far as these people were concerned we now epitomised Jakarta's exploitation of their land. I didn't feel we'd done any disservice to Indonesia by adding this fuel to their grievances, for in the unlikely event of our having been granted permission to climb *Abom*, in Jakarta or elsewhere, we would have been charged a lot more money than this man was asking. Of that I was sure. Then Bruce back-pedalled furiously. 'We didn't know. We had no choice.'

Tabasik's *kepala desa*, the more rational of the two, sat down again .'I understand this. How could you know?' he said. 'But I cannot let you climb the mountain. You must go back to Jakarta and tell them this is our mountain. We should get the money.'

A long lecture on the injustices imposed by the Indonesian government on Irian Jaya followed, punctuated by distracting clicks as the blade leapt out from between his fingers and was pushed back in again. We tried to steer him away from politics, switching our argument to compassionate grounds - we had come so far to climb their beautiful mountain - but time passed without progress. I could see no way out unless we played our ace. It was a dangerous last resort, something that could backfire on us at any point until we were safely on the plane back to London. It was also outright deceit.

Bruce was equally reluctant. 'This could so easily land us in jail, or worse. Who knows who this guy might speak to while we're up the mountain? If it got to the wrong people we'd be screwed.'

We both knew it, but there no longer seemed to be an alternative if we were to go on. Bruce bade the two men disperse the crowd and sit down with us. He spoke in hushed tones. Yes, we knew the political feeling throughout Irian Jaya and, yes, we agreed with him. In fact, one of the reasons behind our journey, the film we were making, the book I was writing, was to reveal their grievances to a wider audience. But without the mountain the film would not be shown, the book would not be published. We were climbing *Abom* for the people of Irian Jaya.

He allowed this revelation to sink in then hit them with the only truthful bit: 'We will be locked up if the authorities get to hear of this.'

It worked. Almost immediately there were smiles all round and we had permission. There was one concession we must make, however: our friends from Aliryi were seen to have done well out of us and it was time for some new men to lighten our cash burden.

I was sad to see the boys go: they had been one of the best things to happen to this expedition. We promised to try to send some photographs and watched them depart for Sumtamun before we set off in the opposite direction with our new head porter, Simsun, and four others.

20 February
We left Biblangda, the next village and the last before the mountain, with eleven companions.

'What's going on now?' wailed Bruce, when it had become clear that none of them were planning to head back. 'What is this? Some kind of circus?'

In addition to the paid up crew of five we had a further three men, one woman, a boy of about twelve, an old man, two piglets and three dogs. All carried bags full of taro. Bruce and I were going to climb a mountain and God alone knew what this lot were planning to do. I didn't mind though: it was a beautiful day and at last we had passed the final village. No more crowds of curious onlookers, no more cramped nights amid a tangle of limbs, no more compulsion to reveal that urine freezes in five minutes in Greenland. I was in high-spirits and our travelling circus made a charming sight.

As we walked out of the village the only concern I felt was for Bruce. He has been taking the anti-biotic metranidazole for several days now in a last effort to defeat whatever is attacking him but he still appears weak and listless. I know him well enough to understand that if he says he's ill, he **is** ill. I also know that I will not be able to stop him pushing himself to the limit on the mountain, let alone delay the start of the climb. I pray the drug will work but neither of us thinks that his symptoms tally with those normally tackled by it. It's a long shot.

By mid-afternoon we had reached our favourite river once again. When last we saw it, the Eilanden was a ferocious obstacle due only to its width. Here it was barely twenty-five yards wide but with the power and roar of a grade-five whitewater-rafting challenge. We were delighted to find the first, proper, rattan suspension bridge of the journey, stretched between two huge boulders. It consisted merely of two strands of rattan for handholds, with a third, the footway, suspended below by regularly spaced split bamboo ties. I spent some time filming, crossing back and forth to capture first the troupe crossing, then, with the head-camera, my own careful footsteps and handholds, until one of the support strands snapped with a mettle-testing 'twang', indicating that I would be foolish to push my luck.

As soon as we had eaten and everyone had got bored with climbing in and out of our bivi-bags, Bruce went to bed. I was not in the mood for fireside scrutiny, or for sleep, so went to the edge of the river to star-gaze. After a while Simsun and Albias came out to join me and ask if I was married and had children. '*Belum.*' Not yet. I gave the standard answer to the most commonly asked question.

'*Kok?*' Why?

The question took me aback. On this journey so far, no-one had asked me to explain that. The answer would require a lengthy explanation on the differences between our respective lives and substantially more Indonesian than usual. I launched into the startling revelation that although here I appeared to be a wealthy man, at home I had next to nothing. I found, to my surprise, that I had picked up more vocabulary than I had realised. I could not, I said, simply get up one morning and decide to build myself a house, or disappear into the forest to clear myself some land and gather the food already growing there. There were too many people in my country, too little land, and it was too cold to get away with wearing just a dried vegetable. I explained the principle of the nine-to-five lifestyle and the constant struggle to make money that defined life in the West. I could not yet afford a wife and children, I concluded.

We stood in silence for a while, stunned, and they retreated to their hut.

'I heard all that. Your vocabulary's really good now.' Bruce enthused when I made to climb into my bag.

'Thanks.'

'What were you trying to tell them, though? I lost you after you'd built a house.'

21 February

This morning there was no immediate hurry. Simsun informed us that a great gathering of food was under-way, then disappeared into the forest. We had breakfast in bed, discussing various possible routes up the mountain. Stored on the camera's memory card are several shots of the south face for this purpose and while we can only view these on the tiny screen there does seem to be a route that holds promise. The second spur appears to hit the main face at a higher altitude than the others, about half a mile to the right of the summit, and there is also a suggestion that, where it does so, there is a break in the otherwise straight line along the top of the cliffs. The spur itself hides from us the final climb to the top of these cliffs and we won't know more until we get there, but it must offer more chance of success than the horror visible to the left and right. The grey cliffs run sheer and unbroken from one side of the screen to the other like a scaled-up version of Cape Town's Table Mountain.

From the top of those cliffs I estimate it's a drop of at least fifteen hundred feet to the highest line of sparse, grassy vegetation where the slope eases by a few degrees for a 3,000ft drop to the tree-line. The pictures were taken from too far away to show any surface detail, but the vegetated lower slope looks equally, if not more, treacherous than the layered strata lines of the naked rock above. Both, to me at least, look beyond the scope of the equipment we carry. For some time I have tried not to think about climbing equipment because we barely have any: a dozen karabiners, a selection of slings from which to make harnesses, two abseiling devices, eight prussic-loops, and a 50-metre, static rope. We have none of the kit you see dangling from the belts of those who know what they are doing: no cams, no nuts, no pitons, no drill or hammer, not even a dynamic rope to absorb the impact of a fall.

'Oh, yeah, and no helmets,' Bruce reminded me gravely, fiddling with the camera.

'Mountaineering 'greats', the likes of Mallory, they didn't have stretchy ropes, did they?' I was seeking reassurance – a rock-climbing guru I had quizzed at home had emphasised that we should not climb on static ropes.

'No, but they reckon Mallory's rope snapped.' Bruce laughed.

Staring at the little screen I felt out of my depth, yet strangely confident. At the top of that spur we would find a way up those cliffs. 'We're going to do this,' I said, suddenly certain of it.

Hours later, as we waded through another swamp, yet more people joined the circus: an old woman who attached herself to the back of the line and a young man who bounded up to the front and introduced himself as Malisin. He was from the village of Jewp, he told us, and had come to help.

'Thank you very much, Malasin, but you should know we have no money to pay you.'

'Oh, I don't want money. My *kepala desa* told me I must come.'

'So everyone in Jewp knows - the grapevine's working well. I can picture our prison cell already,' Bruce remarked airily.

We now have eight unpaid extras. There's no way we can discover how far they intend to accompany us until we know where they think they're taking us, and to what degree that contravenes or matches our own plan to climb the second spur. Simsun is clear only on the fact that the path we are now on leads all the way to Bime, the first village on the other side of the mountains, well over a week away. To do so it must climb over a pass somewhere between the Yamin and Mandala massifs.

During the first rest stop we consulted the map. From the likely position of the pass the summit of our mountain would present no more challenge than a lengthy uphill slog, cutting a path until we are past the tree-line, then trekking up the ridge until we reach the highest point.

'Look at all the food they're carrying. They must be planning to take us all the way round, all the way to the top!' Bruce was pessimistic.

'Piglets and all?'

There was simply no point in arguing with them. We would wait until we reached the second spur and start climbing regardless.

'They've been told to help us. They won't have any choice but to follow,' I pointed out.

A GPS reading this evening showed we had only covered two and a half kilometres on the map. The so-called *'jalan ke* Bime' (path to Bime) is evidently not much travelled: it had to be almost completely re-cut and in places re-routed by the sizeable advance team working flat out in front of us, erecting log walkways around any vertical traverses almost before we got there.

When it began to rain with real intent we all squeezed under a small overhang and attempted to roll cigarettes with wet hands and soggy papers.

'We'll stop here,' Simsun announced, with authority.

'No *pondok*?' I enquired.

'*Belum*! Not yet.'

22 February

The old man, the boy, and two of the dogs did not leave with us this morning. Clasping both my hands in his the old man spoke rapidly in his native tongue. Then he let go with one hand to mime a long fall and wagged a finger to tell me that this was something I should avoid.

'He will ask his ancestors to help you.' Simsun translated the ongoing instructions.

The boy requested a cigarette then ran off after him.

In drab weather we began climbing away from the river to skirt a sheer-sided gorge. It was steep and loose underfoot, requiring both hands whenever I wasn't helping a pig over each fresh obstacle to squeals of indignation. Tail quivering with excitement, it was more intent on rooting out goodies in the dirt and was constantly under my feet. Seeing my difficulty one of the women, Ebola, popped it with the other into her string bag.

Simsun dropped back to wait for us at a barely discernible junction of paths. '*Jalan ke* Bime,' he announced, pointing northwards along the one that had not been cleared.

Hopes soaring, we pointed up hill towards the sound of chopping. 'And this one?'

'Old hunting trail for *cuscus*. There are three *pondoks* higher up.'

We could not believe our luck: there was a path of sorts up the only spur we had seen as being feasible. Not only had we thought we would have a fight on our hands at this moment, but neither of us had relished the prospect of cutting a trail from scratch up a slope like this. I was filled with excitement. 'Bruce, we're going to do this!'

Just above the junction we stopped again as the two women made a cache of the taro they carried and prepared to return to the village. They implored us to be careful and I began to wonder if I should not be feeling a bit more nervous about what was to come. Did they know something we didn't I, wondered aloud?

'No,' Bruce said, as we watched their backs disappearing down the path, the piglets tussling with each other for space in the string bag. 'They only know we have problems staying upright.'

We kept to an ultra-slow pace up to the first of three higher *pondoks* at 2300 metres, conserving energy, grateful that the hard work of chopping undergrowth and branches at face level and above was being done for us. The *pondok*, a tiny affair, was in a sad-state of disrepair. Enough roof had survived to preserve the frame beneath though, and as we put the finishing touches to our sleeping quarters there was already a noisy drying session going on inside - the circus might have lost many of its cast but the party is not over yet. There isn't enough room inside for another two so, having hung up our clothes in there for a thorough smoking, we have crawled into our bivi-bags and are waiting for our ration of baked taro to mash up with the last of the vegetable chilli.

Lent a bit of Western flavour, these dry tubers are transformed into the most delicious meal, but there's never enough. Eating as slowly as possible, eyeing with relish each loaded spoonful, curling the flavour around my mouth, dreading the clank of my spoon hitting the bottom, and wiping the metal spotless with a grubby finger, I try to visualise my tin mug as a huge pot. Bruce is incapable of holding back and wolfs the pathetic amount straight down.

23 February

Bruce felt better on waking than he has for weeks. He could not have chosen a more wonderful day to rediscover his old self.

The sun stayed out all morning, affording us occasional views through the trees of the south face and summit, and the rare pleasure of walking through a moss forest under a clear sky. Minuscule droplets of water clinging to the delicate stems of the moss glistened and sparkled like a billion diamonds set in the subtle shades of green and ochre, as if at the whim of the most extravagant gardener. Between narrow arches, tunnels and short, vertical climbs the path became a shallow indentation barely wider than the sole of my boot, meandering between rocks so thickly covered with moss as to look like great semi-spherical sponges. The little trail looked as if someone had rolled a heavy cannonball down the mountainside to provide a highway for whatever that had left the little piles of droppings I found at regular intervals. It was just too beautiful to imagine that man had ever been there, like an undisturbed coral reef.

The archways and tunnels required some *parang* work to get through and the pace was slow enough for me to become so absorbed in the scene that I forgot how treacherous it was. When they got tired of finding me embedded to the waist in what had appeared to be a solid surface, struggling to free my legs, the men bringing up the rear eventually overtook, allowing me to drop back and feel as if I were completely alone.

At just over three-thousand metres, when I caught up with the leaders again, the rotten frame of a sizeable *pondok* was lying on the ground and the first poles of a new one were going up. At this height the pandanus leaves used to make a watertight roof were becoming scarce. Dasok and Malasin were hard at work with the materials they had collected so far, their T-shirts and shorts discarded in favour of penis gourds to keep them dry.

From far below came the unmistakable crash of a large tree hitting the ground, followed by shouts. Simsun appeared out of the bushes. '*Cuscus*,' he said, with relish. 'Dog finds *cuscus* up a tree, men cut down the tree, dog catches *cuscus*.'

It wasn't a *cuscus* but a Daria's tree kangaroo, the size of a koala bear but with a much smaller head. In the finished *pondok* we filmed its transition from delightful-looking furry mammal to charred meal. We were offered a roasted foot, claws and all, and a section of intestine. The latter came complete with what would have been tomorrow morning's defecation.

We did get some meat as well but as I watched the skull and bones passed round to be stripped of the last shreds of flesh and marrow I thought of the night we had spent in Bebecleh, when everyone kept waking up because of the cold. It was great that they wasted nothing. In the West we routinely put too much on our plates then throw away what we can't eat.

But they had wasted something and here was an answer to their freezing nights. 'In the thousands of years since they populated these hills no one has ever thought to use the fur for anything,' I said to Bruce. 'It would only take six of those things to make a blanket or cloak that would last for years.'

24 February

Today has brought more of the same: uphill chopping at a slow pace, but this time in thick cloud and continuous drizzle. By mid-afternoon the last sizeable trees were below us. Those men not slashing a way through were foraging for firewood, and suitable leaves for the next roof. Of the last hunting lodge nothing remained but two upright poles standing at either end of a levelled platform in the moss. 'No more *win*, no more *pondok*.' Simsun pointed further up the spur.

This was base camp then, the point to which the men must return each evening if they were to venture further up the mountain. Most were already shivering.

Through occasional thinning of the cloud we could see that another hour's climb would have us well out of the last trees and in a better position to view possible routes in the early morning sunlight. More than that, however, we were both desperate to be left alone. We had not been able to enjoy our own company and just speak English since we left Agats.

What path there was petered out as the heavy limbs and leaves of the forest gave way to sub-alpine heath, with a thick heathery covering dotted with stunted bushes. Nevertheless the going was easier than it had been for days. Where the spur flattened out at just over 3,400 metres before it dropped into a shallow saddle and then another climb, we found the perfect spot: a flat springy mattress bordered by a natural windbreak of taller scrub. It was dripping wet, but our first night without onlookers and alien chatter just had to include a fire. There would not be another chance. Any wood we found above this spot would be even wetter. Perhaps no man had ever before come so far up this spur. Just like the camp we had made with Superman *en route* to the Korowai, on the shingle by the river deep in the forest, this one had about it a kind of purity: free from development, uncontaminated by domesticity, exempt from etiquette. It only lacked a fire.

For once I was happy to let Bruce demonstrate his skills in the fire-lighting department. We differ in technique, but as the self-proclaimed master of that trickiest of camping skills, Bruce's pride, I knew, would keep him blowing on the most meagre sparks until either an inferno was raging or he had passed out.

I made the coffee on a meagre flame.

Long after we had given up and gone to bed, the fire flared up and set light to my penultimate pair of socks.

16 'A STUPENDOUS ABYSS'

25 February

At seven a.m. Simsun and crew, bearing hot taro, joined us just as the clouds moved in on our spur. Until then the big, green wall ahead had not looked any easier but we reckoned to be setting up camp one at the top by the end of the day. In fact it took until two o'clock just to fight our way through the thick bushes and moss infesting the slight dip in the ridgeline and the final climb to the base of the wall, leaving too little time in the torrential rain to attempt a camp higher up.

The ridge had narrowed to a knife-edged arête that required artificial widening before we could establish camp one - slender poles lodged between rocks, then overlaid with leafy branches and moss - but it's a fabulous position. Left again to our own devices we rested on our roll-mats for the remainder of the day, chatting and cooking as a strengthening wind and heavy rain lashed and tore at the gamely resilient basha sheet. On closer examination the green wall, to which one end of the sheet is now tied, appears achievable as an unroped scramble but our tiny platform will be the only thing to stop a fall. We've nicknamed the coming climb, '*Awas*'.

26 February

Bruce slept through the alarm on his watch and we were not under way until five-thirty. In the light of this we decided to conduct a lightweight reconnaissance to the top of *Awas* in the hope of getting some idea, before the clouds took over, of what happened when the spur hit the main face of the mountain. The first two hundred feet were uncomfortably close to vertical, the vegetation soaking and loose. My hands were numb with cold and freezing water ran down the inside of my sleeves and boots. The moss overlay had little grip on the smooth rock beneath and appeared to be held there purely by its own tensile strength. It was very difficult to avoid ripping it, whereupon the whole thing would start tearing away, pulling us off the rockface. It was very frightening. There was nothing for it but to put tremendous amounts of faith into the intermittent tufts of coarse grass and dwarf shrubs, but we had to take great care to spread the load between as many points as possible at any one time. Most could only be used once - we found that out when attempting to follow each other - but the bushes were stronger and more firmly rooted than their slim trunks suggested. A solid barrier of them ran along the top edge of the steepest section. To get through meant losing contact with the face to haul myself up through the branches, consolidating each new position in what felt like mid-air, then slashing with my *parang* a hole above my head through which I had to clamber. Without a *parang*, Bruce followed me through the hole. It was exhausting work but after that the climb became considerably easier, and by eight o'clock the face had narrowed once more to a ridge that could almost be walked. We stopped as the sun emerged from behind *Abom's* south-eastern flank, radiating heat that sent clouds of steam drifting from the moss and our trousers. We wished we had brought the rest of the equipment.

The top of the face blocked any view of what lay ahead. In half-an-hour we would be at the top of the next section but in all likelihood that would also offer no view. Already the valley clouds were storming up the slope towards us. I could almost see the bubbles of thermic air erupting upwards, gathering condensation as they swept over the treetops and into the thinner, colder air. Should we get to the next crest, hoping to beat the cloud for that slim possibility of a view, or take a gamble and go back down for the rest of the kit? One clear view of the junction between our spur and the summit ridge might reveal an impassable barrier, in which case we would have to retreat almost to base camp for an attempt up the valley on our left. Earlier glimpses had shown a deep saddle in the summit ridge at the head of this valley but we had seen it only in silhouette and had grave suspicions about the severity of the cliffs beneath.

The valley to the right was a non-starter. Curving gently to the north-east our spur now offered an excellent view into its depths and all the way to the main face. I sat on the edge, my legs dangling over cloud. We named it 'Long Drop Valley'.

A ridge was bound to offer a greater chance of success but we opted to try for a view anyway and set off in a high-speed scramble to beat the clouds to the next top. We made it in time for a twenty-second glimpse of our spur levelling out as it veered north-eastwards towards the next major climb and beyond to the main face. It didn't tell the full story, but at least we had seen the next obstacle and reckoned we could climb it - the best we could hope for. Once again I felt a surge of confidence that we were following the right route. That we now had to go back down to camp one seemed ludicrous. We cursed ourselves again for having left the kit behind.

'Great leeches, though.' Bruce held up his hands. Like mine they were streaked with blood. 'Here, you've got one on your face.'

It was extraordinary to find leeches up there. What on earth do they live on? The speed with which they bit us compared to their sluggish lowland cousins suggested they were eerily aware that we would be the last meal to drop by for some time.

Enveloped in cloud we descended at once. I wasn't looking forward to negotiating those fragile tufts of grass backwards but was surprised to find the descent easier, until I realised how foolish I was being: buoyed by excitement I was losing all caution, leading the way at a ludicrous pace without stopping to think about our direction. I was trying to follow the slash marks and bootprints of our upward path and lost the trail, then thought we were losing the ridgeline so veered left towards a vague outline momentarily visible in the cloud. It soon became clear that we had come the wrong way. As I peered over the edge of a precipice Bruce confirmed with the GPS that I had been about to pay an impromptu visit to the bottom of Long Drop Valley. We climbed back up and traversed to the right - I had misjudged the speed at which we had arrived at the top of *Awas*. It was a sobering lesson and a great relief to spot the red sheet and the solar panels directly below us.

With my sense of caution now fully alert the last hundred metres proved too much to contemplate so we rigged up an abseil. As I assisted Bruce in spreading the load evenly between four bushes I heard him muttering to himself sarcastically: 'Top-roping and abseiling, lesson number one: always choose a bomb-proof belay. These bloody things aren't even firework proof.'

Wisely he went down it first while, with mounting horror, I examined the damage being done to the bushes, but there were no others to tie on to and therefore I had to go for it, descend as quickly and smoothly as possible, praying loudly all the way and keeping a vague grip on *terra firma*. I registered enthusiastic applause and a chorus of '*Awas, awas!*' from below through the awful whirring of the rope passing through the figure-of-eight descender.

Albias, Dalok and Simsun were waiting for us at camp one, teeth chattering, and thrust taro into our hands. We had planned to depart again immediately but decided to wait until the following morning. It was not the heavy rain so much as the state of the camera batteries. We didn't want to climb with the charging equipment, and the heavy cloud meant that only a trickle charge was being delivered to batteries that had to last three to four days. Miraculously, despite the wind and rain that battered our eyrie all afternoon, they were all fully charged by nightfall.

27 February

Before first light we dismantled camp one, leaving the satellite phone in a waterproof bag and the solar panels lashed to the platform to keep it charged up for any emergency. Within three hours, we had reached the previous day's viewpoint, feeling strong and confident. A surprise was in store.

In the brief glimpse afforded us yesterday the ridge had appeared to level out for at least three-hundred metres before it climbed steeply again. Striding out along this, however, we came to a standstill against a wall of ten-foot bushes. Unimpeded by fallen trees or lack of light they occupied every square inch of space, overhanging the precipice on the right and dropping out of sight over the convex slope to the left. Tough, rough-barked trunks and branches were hooked up and interwoven with those of the next, leaving so little space that a hedgehog would have had difficulty in passing. Getting through it, I thought at the time, was going to be like trying to cross a football stadium filled with coil after coil of barbed wire stacked three high.

I gave silent thanks that I had brought my *parang* and took a swipe at the first branch. It sprang back uninjured. Another swipe. It was still there, slightly maimed. All of my strength went into the third, and it fell. Another three branches to go before I could take the first step forward to tackle the next lot. Fifteen minutes later we had penetrated just a few yards. After an hour I was sweating grimly. We took it in turns. It rained, heavily. Tempers flared when Bruce insisted on giving a talk to camera on this unusual mountaineering phenomenon only to have the beleaguered instrument, despite its rain cover, flash the water-droplet symbol and clunk ominously to a halt. We already had hours of 'chopping' footage but now there was no fire to dry out the camera before the finale of our film. I transferred my anger to the bushes.

We began to climb out of the dip and from the clutches of this hellish arbour, as my watch showed four o'clock. It had taken seven hours to go just a few hundred metres. The ridge narrowed as it climbed once more, the gaps between bushes gradually more negotiable. There was no time to attempt the next face so we found a dip in the mossy overlay and dug out a campsite with hands and *parang*, rigging the basha sheet as low as possible out of the stinging wind that whipped over the edge of the precipice on our right.

28 February

Bruce must have been as knackered as I was – he slept through his alarm again.

A beautiful but cold morning began with an unpleasant frenzy but the speed at which we broke camp was due more to the temperature of the saturated clothing and boots we had left outside our bivi-bags overnight than to the fact that we had lost an hour.

The remainder of this section of the ridge posed no great difficulty but ended in the face we had glimpsed two days before. On closer examination it was a stepped slope of ledges and steep banks, russet and green, dotted with occasional stunted bushes, like the lower slopes of a Scottish peak before the heather. It was treacherous, though, with more fragile moss clinging to smooth rock. I took two falls, landing heavily the second time some five metres below. The relatively soft landing did little to restore my bruised confidence. Twice I had to ask the more proficient Bruce to find a belay point and throw a rope down to me, then used a prussic to secure my ascent. This cost us time, as did having to dry out the camera as soon as we hit some sunlight. By the time we had negotiated the next ridgeline and arrived at another face the cloud had once again enveloped the scene.

We left the rucksacks at the foot of a cliff-line that disappeared into the mist to the left and scouted around the broken ground on the right for a route up, climbing through a cleft in the rock that kept us in line with the continuation of the spur. The surface was horribly loose: Bruce's every move sent showers of stone down so that I had to wait until he was at the top. There, the ground changed from moss, rock and grass to an extraordinary moonscape of flat, naked limestone dissected by linear fissures of anything up to two metres deep. There was more chance of a decent campsite below so we opted for a quick reconnaissance before going back to the rucksacks. Razor-sharp ridges and fossilised seashells sliced chunks from the soles of my boots and from my fingers but the going was fast and easy up a gentle incline cluttered with massive boulders. In a deep, square-sided trench that could have been scoured out by a mechanical digger, we took shelter from the drizzle blowing across the slope and checked the GPS. We had passed the 4200-metre mark, and were 500 metres below the summit. There couldn't be much left between where we were and the summit ridge but there was still no sign of the final climb. To the right there was still a precipice and another to the left.

We kept going in almost zero visibility. It was like a navigational assessment to which the Army had once subjected me in Norway.

When the next obstacle appeared we were almost right underneath it. A great, jagged, black profile zoomed out of the cloud then vanished just as quickly, like a gargantuan tousled head peering down at us through smoke, then recoiling in horror. It certainly looked high enough to take us to the summit ridge.

There was not a great choice of alternative activities for what little remained of the daylight so we hung around under a boulder smoking damp cigarettes and waiting for a better view. All was revealed just as we were about to return to the rucksacks. Steep but not vertical, it was a big, lumpy face of jutting angular rock perhaps a hundred metres high and narrowing to a point at the top. Tufts of grass and moss infested every crack and crevice. It didn't look so bad but it wasn't alone. As I looked up the blanket of cloud behind it was whipped away to reveal another peak towering over the first, clean and grey against a patch of blue sky. Set back a little further the summit ridge swept behind from left to right, almost horizontal. The picture faded and was gone. We both swore, then lapsed into a shocked silence.

'Ooh, *bahaya*! Danger,' I said eventually, mimicking Simsun's reaction to the face above camp one.

'We go lightweight,' said Bruce, with a bit more thought and a note of finality. 'Climbing gear, camera, and just enough kit to survive a night out if necessary.'

'What?' There was no way that, having got up that thing, I was coming down again without staying for a good look round in the morning.

'This is not a mountain to mess around with. A storm could come in.'

'So what? We get wet! I'm soaking anyway. I'm all in favour of ditching the rucksacks but I think we should plan to stay up there. We're not talking Everest - we'll still be lower than most base camps, and we're on the equator.'

'If there's one thing I've learnt it's never to underestimate a mountain. People die on hills a lot smaller than this.'

'Please don't patronise me. We know it can't get much below freezing up there.'

We argued all the way down, until we realised that we had lost the rucksacks, it would be dark in half-an-hour and we had underestimated the mountain. The GPS told us exactly what direction to go in but it was remarkably difficult to find the route we had taken around the cliffs under which the luggage lay. I stumbled upon another, and in so doing found a perfect camp three: a small cave narrowing like a windsock, but large enough at the entrance to fit two bivi-bags on adventurously uncomfortable ground.

The low ceiling is covered in a thick layer of whitish, gritty slime that has oozed from the rock - stalactites in foetal form. In an effort to avoid brushing against it - whereupon showers of it drop accurately down necks and into cooking arrangements - we have been waddling around on our haunches. Several piles of droppings suggest we are not necessarily alone.

2 March
At some point during the night a furious screeching just outside my bivi-bag woke me. Someone (of about the size of a Chihuahua) wanted either to leave their home, or enter it after a busy day on the slopes and was not best pleased to find two sarcophagi in the doorway.

For once we were up at the right time, well before daybreak. It was far too dark and miserable to consider anything but a good breakfast. The sun does not hang around at five degrees of latitude, though, and the sky was already turning a magnificent dark cobalt as I wolfed down my chicken and pasta. As soon as the treachery of the landscape was uncloaked we climbed the easier route revealed by the previous day's incompetence, reaching Bahaya One, as the first of the next two climbs was now called, before the sun had. At its foot we cached the rucksacks between a trio of boulders and secured the red basha sheet over the top, both as a visible marker and to catch any rainfall. As a final touch I activated a chemical light-stick in case we had to find them in the dark. The instructions on the packet had rubbed off and neither of us could remember how long they worked for but it seemed a clever thing to do. Bruce carried the rope slung over both shoulders and the grappling-hook at his belt. The camera was wrapped in layers of waterproofing inside his bum-bag. I carried a rope-bag packed with a bivi-bag, half a roll-mat, a silver-foil survival blanket, two days' worth of food and the cooker. The karabiners on our improvised harnesses jangled professionally with every movement.

'Cool,' said Bruce, when we were ready. 'How does my rope look?'

'You're the epitome of exploration.'

'Excellent. Let's go.'

Bahaya One was an easy scramble over and between jutting rocks and up mossy fissures. At the top there was more of the flat, segmented rock; a wide platform dropping very slightly for fifty metres to a short ramp of scree running around the foot of Bahaya Two. The silence struck me. Wisps of cloud were bouncing harmlessly along the sunlit cliffs of the summit ridge above but I could neither feel nor hear any wind. Brittle shards of loose rock crunched under our boots. Bordered on three sides by precipices and looked upon only by *Abom* and the gods, it was like a high altar of the Incas with all but its history scoured clean.

Bahaya Two reared up some 180-metres above us, a bulge in the summit ridge and perhaps the last hurdle. It looked daunting and technical. It wasn't smooth rock, however: several fissures looked as if they might provide a route up. I fancied a stratum line that disappeared off to the left about half-way up. It looked like an easy traverse but we ruled it out as it went round into the next gully where the drop below might become mesmerising. We decided to go straight up.

'You lead, I'll wear the head-cam,' I volunteered, before Bruce did.

We had discarded the useless baseball cap as a camera platform, adapting my head-torch to take the tiny lens. I carried the bum-bag with the main camera slung over my shoulders on top of the rope-bag.

The knowledge that there was a microphone just inches above my forehead made me suddenly aware of how heavily I was breathing in the thin air. I had been much higher than this several times before but marvelled at those who had climbed to twice this height without supplementary oxygen. I was also aware of how dehydrated I was. It was eight-thirty and there did not seem to be nearly so much cloud forming as there had been on previous mornings. I wondered vaguely if this would be a problem - a day without rain would be a longed-for miracle but we might be in trouble if there was no snow or water at the top. My tongue was almost stuck to the roof of my mouth already.

I let Bruce free-climb the eight or so metres up to the first fissure. For reasons of weight we had brought no rock-gripping gadgetry to provide security and, despite an abundance of obvious handholds, I could see nothing to loop a sling round. He reported down: 'There's still nothing to belay on to, but it's great climbing. The rock's solid and really grippy. Follow me up!'

Grippy? Surely such a word was not to be found in the lexicon of real mountaineering. But any doubts I had vanished as soon as I was on the rock. He was right, it was grippy, and there was a huge choice of holds. I was even able to dismiss most of those that were painfully sharp. By any standards this was, I supposed grudgingly, an easy climb but the height and total absence of safety measures made it a serious task. I was surprised by how unperturbed I felt. Even when the second fissure proved too narrow for the bags I carried, forcing me to traverse right and on to rock directly above Long Drop Valley, I felt none of the bowel slackening, knee-trembling terror that had hampered so many army climbs in Wales. I pulled out a loose stone and watched it bounce, then spin out into a patch of wispy cloud, enjoying the ripple of excitement when no further sound emanated from its 1,100-metre descent. This was adventure. Here, far from anywhere, far from help, my life was hanging from my fingertips. My dry, cracked hands looked capable and strong. I spoke casually to Bruce above me and to the camera on my head, overwhelmingly confident that we were going to conquer the south face.

17 HIGH AND LOW

2 March (continued...)

When the cassette reached its end after forty minutes I was standing on a ledge just below the top. Minutes later I swung my leg over the lip and looked left and right. We were on the summit ridge and nothing could stop us now. I felt like shaking Bruce's hand there and then but cloud was swirling around us now and there was still almost a mile to go.

Running north-westwards towards the summit, the ridge in front dropped down into the deep saddle we had seen from base camp, then climbed back up into wispy cloud, edging its way past a huge slope of scree crossed horizontally with thin, equally spaced ledges of solid rock, like a broad stairway all but covered with sand. To the right, a vast expanse of the flat-topped, fissured rock sloped away at thirty degrees into yet more cloud, which was now sweeping up the north-eastern flank. 'We're going to lose all visibility in a minute. I reckon we stick to the ridge,' said Bruce, as we derigged the camera and evened up the loads again.

I grunted in agreement, but once we were on our way the ridge became impossibly knife-edged, with a tremendous 'axecleft' fissure barring forward progress. We were forced to head diagonally right and off the high ground, picking a way down to cross the chasm where its edges opened out and it lost its drama. It looked as though in upheaval from the seabed to 4,700 metres this vast chunk of oceanic plate had almost arrived intact, only to snap in two at the last minute, the fault line searing across the rock from the north to stop just a few feet short of ripping the mountain's south face apart. The rift widened, its sides becoming less steep as it plunged down towards the northern jungle.

The scree beneath our feet as we climbed up the opposite side was bizarre. Perfectly even slopes of wafer thin shards up to four inches long, like discarded knife-blades tipped from the top by the truckload and extremely awkward to walk up. Each footstep crunched noisily, triggering miniature landslides that tried to drag my boots with them, spilling over the next ledge with a delicate tinkling sound. A prehistoric flint-knapper would have struggled to achieve edges like these. Every time my feet were swept away and I put my hands out for support they came away polka-dotted with bright flecks of new blood. It was such hard work climbing the stuff that we veered away from the planned line of ascent to where the lines of scree were narrower and fewer, opting instead to tackle a succession of five to ten metre crags. These were easier on the legs and lungs but no less murderous on the hands. Broken seashells now attacked, stabbing out from every piece of rock like smashed bottles embedded in the cement of a perimeter wall. I remarked to Bruce that to fall here would be to die the death of a thousand cuts long before you hit the bottom. Other than that we barely spoke, picking our own routes over the rock, alternately leading each other through the wandering cloud and startlingly bright patches of sunlight. The only sounds were the crunch of each step and the dry rasp of my breath. I longed for a drink.

We regained the summit ridge at the same time as we crested the top of the scree slope. Bruce was there before me, and took the camera out of its waterproof wrappings. Beyond him the ridgeline meandered onwards to a high point some four hundred metres distant. 'That's got to be it! Sit on that rock ahead and say something to camera.' He held out the radio mike.

I sat on the edge of the next bulge in the ridgeline, grinning back at him across the abyss and babbling something about the uncertainty of months dropping away because there it was, at last, nothing left between us and it. Before moving off again I waited for him to pack away the camera and catch me up. I wanted Bruce to reach the summit first. Or perhaps we would take it together. Whatever, this had been his dream, and he ought to be the first Briton to stand on it. I would not have been here but for him and felt overwhelming gratitude.

As it was, I felt helplessly drained of energy over the last few hundred paces and he was sitting on the summit filming me as I arrived. Elation, joy, relief - on top of the world. It was a feeling like no other I had ever experienced. We shook hands for the camera then I shook his again, and had to turn away to hide a sudden welling of tears. I peered over into the 'stupendous abyss' that had so captured our imaginations since we had read of it in that ancient book and laughed with delight. We had done it. We were at an almost celestial height, above the clouds, above everything. And yet this mountain was a mere pimple. What must Edmund Hillary and Tenzing Norgay have felt?

'It's two o'clock already. Let's stay the night up here,' said Bruce.

'Good boy!' If we had been wet and cold it might have been a different story, a single bivi-bag too grim to contemplate. But the sun was still with us and the problem of water had been solved: the northern side of the mountain from the summit was an almost completely flat-sided slab, dropping for well over a mile down to the tree-line and a small circular lake. The rock was riven with deep fissures and holes, many of which had snow visible in their depths. We hunted for the most accessible of these and I climbed into it to fill up a bag that Bruce hauled up on the rope and set about melting. Thirst pacified, we split up to explore.

From the summit pinnacle I watched Bruce leaping over the cracks some distance below, a tiny figure scurrying about, disappearing, then reappearing between occasional outcrops. The silence was huge, as if sound itself had never existed here. Every noise I made - a crunch of rock or a rattle of tin-mug - was swallowed as if by a vacuum or black hole. It was eerily unreal, another world, the sounds I made the only link connecting me to the immensity of it, the only assurance that I was actually there. Twice I thought I could see the ice we had been so disappointed to miss. Strangely, it was well below the summit but I was too mesmerised by the glacial shimmer to take any notice of this trifling incongruity and twice set off to investigate. It was just the light playing tricks.

When it began to snow gently we found a tiny overhang under which to melt snow and cook. I went off in search of somewhere that was not at thirty degrees for the bivi-bag. The snow in the bottom of our 'well' might have made the most comfortable surface but the cold down there was of the kind that seeps through every defence, damp and chilling. I became a bit preoccupied with other holes I came across, dropping rocks into them and delighting in the length of time it took for any sound to come out. Some were very, very deep.

The spot I found for our sleeping quarters was on top of the slab. Just big enough for our bivi-bag, it was in the lee of a small outcrop that would shelter us against the developing wind from the north, but only that outcrop would prevent us rolling away in the night, helplessly zipped into our own body-bag. I smashed the shells and razor-like ridges in the rock that would otherwise go straight through the roll-mat and mutilate the Gore-Tex bag, and attempted to even out the sloping platform with handfuls of gravel, but there was little that could be done. It was going to be the most miserable night yet.

We crawled inside as soon as it was dark, and froze. Not a millimetre of insulating air lay between our two bodies and the thin walls. It was only possible to lie on our sides facing the same way, one arm deadened against the lumpy rock. From outside we must have looked like a tightly swollen maggot impaled on a spike. From inside it looked worse. To retain all possible heat the door was zipped completely shut, only the 'breathable' Gore-Tex allowing in a fresh supply of oxygen. I was amazed to find that the fabric could cope with two pairs of lungs, especially at almost five thousand metres but it swiftly became apparent that it could only do so when we were breathing deep and slow. Even the effort of a few spoken words sent oxygen levels plummeting. Changing position brought us near to unconsciousness. After each movement we struggled to control our breathing in the thin air, growing rapidly more hypoxic until one of us wrenched open the zip and sucked in gasping lungfuls. The space-blanket stayed on only long enough to produce little puddles of condensation. It ended up wrapped damply around our feet where we could not reach it. Our teeth chattered.

'I think I'm getting hypothermic,' said Bruce.

'So am I. I can't f-f-feel my feet.'

'Th-th-there's only one thing for it - we're g-g-g-going to have to share bodily warmth.'

I remembered dreading this survival technique throughout the recruit-training period of my military career. The idea of stripping off and climbing into a sleeping-bag with another man who'd been running around the hills in the same clothes for over a week had been repellent, an absolute last resort. But now, I had to concede, we were already half-way there: the atmosphere inside the bivi-bag was hardly less than rancid. And Bruce was right - we were shivering uncontrollably.

I wriggled outside to zip our two fleeces into their Gore-Tex outers, pull the sleeves inside out then zip the two garments together. Before I squirmed back in, I stripped off down to the waist and handed my shirts in to Bruce, who arranged them over the floor with his own. It took an age to manoeuvre the jackets over the top of us as a draught-free double duvet, and then we hugged, all night. It wasn't fun, but it worked - so well that we could keep the door open a couple of inches.

I slept in the brief intervals between wrestling bouts, waking each time a subconscious alarm sounded the news that my arm would have to be amputated if denied blood for a minute longer. At the first sign of daylight I was out of there. Bruce remained within, pushing his luck. 'I haven't slept at all. Leave me your jacket - thanks!' He tried to zip the door shut while I struggled into my shirts but there was no way he was getting away with that.

While I was brewing up soup on the summit I found an old coffee jar wedged into a crack in the rock. Breathless with excitement I unscrewed the lid, expecting to find a note, perhaps left by the 1959 expedition. It was half full of black paint, dried up. Nearby was a dried-up paintbrush. I scoured the surrounding rock for a painted message or date, but wind, rain and time are scrupulous cleaners. Neither of us had thought to bring up something with which to leave our mark but I had a tiny Union Jack on a stick - the sort the Queen must get so bored of seeing. We'd planned to take home a photograph of the two of us standing on the summit, resplendent in penis-gourds with flags poking out of the top and fluttering proudly, but Bruce's gourd had been crushed and his flag left behind. I performed the ceremony alone in a flurry of snow. We left the flag in a medicine pot next to the coffee jar - the first British ascent.

Snow-laden squalls whistled over the top of the summit pinnacle as we crouched in its lee, looking down into the 'stupendous abyss' and eating breakfast. The sky was heavily overcast with high stratus, and a bank of lower cloud was advancing up the slab from the north. No cloud was yet forming over Biblangda but we had had our clear day and were not going to get another. Map in hand I gazed wistfully through the layers of vapour at the jungle rolling away to the northern horizon, as featureless from up here as a plantation of pine, and cursed the fact that we were no longer going there. I was looking down into areas that had never been properly surveyed. 'Relief Data Incomplete', announced the map. 'MEF believed not to exceed 7400 feet'; 'Generally Forest Covered'. Only major rivers spotted from the air and two villages had been jotted down on a plain white background. Using outstretched fingers I measured roughly the distance we had walked since leaving Sera Dala and transposed the same on to a northerly bearing from where we sat. My filthy fingernail landed squarely in the middle of a patch so white and unblemished it might have represented the Arctic icecap.

'I wonder if the jungle in there is any different from that in the south,' I said absently.

'Harrer, and the guys in the film said that leeches dropped from the trees like rain, remember?'

At ten o'clock when the last camera battery had almost died we headed back along the ridge. Visibility had dropped to less than thirty metres before we had gone far. Rain turned the rock black.

I pulled up my hood and above the hammering of raindrops heard my breathing suddenly amplified, reminding me of my own fragility in this place. Suddenly I was no longer thrilled to be where I was. I wanted to be down: there was a chocolate bar in Wamena with my name on it, and after that a stool in a Balinese pool-bar. There were no 'unknowns' left, only surprises and, in all probability, unpleasant ones. The grey forms looming out of the choking murk looked surreal and unfamiliar, challenging recognition as if mocking our ability to escape. It should be easy, I told myself: follow the ridge until it drops towards the axe-cleft fissure, bear diagonally left across the scree slope until you reach the bottom, then climb diagonally right to pick up the ridgeline again. No problem. I determined not to think about Bahaya Two until we got there.

The edge of the fault-line came and went. We moved quickly, glissading down the slopes of scree, calling out the names we had given to a few recognisable features as they appeared reassuringly out of the gloom: 'Here are the gate posts!'

Bruce consulted the GPS. 'They're supposed to be thirty metres over there but, yeah, agreed, that's them.' We both knew about the margin of error in the GPS system.

'Flintstones cave!'

'Got it!'

It was going well. As we climbed the opposite side of the fault-line, our old footprints were briefly visible across a short section of more scree. The ridge was just on our right again. Any minute now we would be at the top of Bahaya Two. I stopped dead. 'Bruce, we've come too far!' As well as the 'stupendous abyss' on my right there was one in front of me too. 'I don't recognise this.'

'Neither do I, but this thing says Bahaya Two is fifteen metres...' he oriented himself, '...that way.' He pointed straight over the cliff in front of me.

I peered over the edge. 'Mate, we did not come up this!' Not only did the cliff itself look horrendous but the ground at the bottom was not right: a small flattish area of what looked like rubble was dimly visible. It might just be the spot where I had donned the head camera, I thought, except that the orientation was all wrong. Our direction of climb had been perpendicular to the summit ridge, but if that climb was back over my right shoulder where I thought it should be then what the hell was this doing here? The cliffs of the summit ridge south-east of Bahaya Two and our spur had continued in an almost straight line...or had they?

'Well, where do you reckon it is, then?' Bruce sounded irritable.

'Over here.' I strode across to the cliff on our right.

'Oh.' It dropped a very, very long way. I couldn't see the bottom for cloud. Nothing made sense any more. I turned a slow 360 degrees but nothing registered. Fleeting gaps in the cloud kept attracting my attention, like lifelines thrown and retracted. Black shapes and outlines filled my head with a jumble of images that would not compute. Apart from knowing which way was south I felt disoriented, a horrible sensation.

Bruce was uncertain, too. We retraced our steps as far as the footprints we had passed earlier but it didn't help: we ended up back at the top of that black cliff again. He brought up the position of the rucksack cache with the GPS and computed the bearing between it and us. My compass pointed over the black cliff.

'Bollocks!'

'Remember, always trust your compass,' Bruce joked.

'I do trust my compass. I've just never before had one insist that I go over a cliff.'

'Well, you have now.'

'I'm still not sure about this.'

'Neither am I.'

We found a good route but had to abseil parts. The rock streamed with water that ran in rivulets between the seashells and dripped over each ledge like an Oriental bead screen.

'At least it's still grippy!' Bruce called.

Half-way down there was a wide ledge running all the way

around to the right. He landed on it triumphantly. 'This is the ledge you wanted to follow on the way up!'

'It is not the ledge I wanted to follow! That ledge ran round to the axe-cleft fissure. This one runs out to the south face.'

We scouted along it for a route to the bottom.

'Look at that big white scar. Surely you remember it?'

I really wanted to remember it. 'No, I don't.' As far as I was concerned we were abseiling irretrievably into a bloody great hole. I had visions of not being able to climb out again and of being trapped above 4,000 metres with no food and a bivi-bag designed for one.

When I reached the bottom of the last abseil Bruce had disappeared into the mist. I delayed flicking the rope to release the sling at the top from its tenuous hold round a 'sticky-out' bit of rock - the climbing lexicon certainly didn't include that one either - until he had reappeared with good news. We might want to climb up it. The cloud refused to part even for an orienting instant, but emitted a muffled shout.

'This is a spur. It's got to be the right one. Bring the rope.'

Across a flattish area of fine scree there was an unruly pile of boulders. We found shelter from the driving rain behind one and consulted the GPS. It said we were going in the right direction and only a linear fifty metres from the rucksacks, straight over the edge of the last boulder visible silhouetted against the cloud. We had a look, the cloud parted obligingly, and there they were, the red sheet clearly visible far below. We were now on top of Bahaya One and had indeed climbed down Bahaya Two. Bruce began to speak. I was sure it wasn't going to be 'I told you so,' but I cut him short anyway. 'Yes, yes, yes!'

I never did work out exactly where we came down in relation to where we climbed up. I have only the image of Bahaya Two from our ascent and the rock-face we descended does not exist in that image.

The climb down to the cache was as easy in reverse, and having decanted the water collected in the sheet and hurriedly repacked we were off again. Going further than camp three was now out of the question. The day had crept by, it was already after three o'clock, and I was in no mood to tackle the grassy face I had fallen off a few days before. Arriving at the top of the crumbling section we had now negotiated three times already there seemed to be a shortage of holds down our usual route. They had all come out. Bruce went left, I went right, to look for another way. I found one but it was slow work pulling off a thick blanket of moss to find the rock beneath before making each move. I called to Bruce but there was no answer. Evidently he had found his own round the corner.

Suddenly a piercing cry rang out from my right. I turned my head just in time to catch, in the corner of my eye, an indistinct silhouette, arms flailing wildly, as it catapulted over the edge of the spur. There was no further sound, just the wind, and the rain on my hood. I clung to the rock.

We had looked over that edge on the way up. It was at least eight hundred metres straight down into Long Drop Valley. It hit me like a hammer blow. Bruce was dead.

18 A RAPID DESCENT

2 March (continued…)

I had about five moves to make before I reached the bottom.

'Shit, shit, shit!' The word reverberated around my head as I tore off the moss in strips, mind racing away from the task. I didn't want to look into Long Drop Valley. I knew I wouldn't see anything: there was nothing to stop him down there. Perhaps I could abseil down. No, he had the rope. I jumped the last bit and strode towards the edge, unclipping my pack-straps as I went.

Something in front stopped me in my tracks. It took a second to grasp that I was looking at Bruce, coming towards me from behind the rock saying 'There's no getting that back.'

I just stared. He giggled.

'You ____!' My knees almost buckled with relief. 'You complete ____!'

'Chill out! At least the main camera wasn't in it.' He didn't have a clue what he'd just put me through.

'I thought that was you going over the edge!'

'Oh - sorry!' He giggled again.

It was only his rucksack that had gone over. What I had thought were flailing arms must have been the waist straps. He told me what had happened. One of his shoulder straps had broken as he made the last heavy step on to the gentle slope at the bottom of his climb. As the pack had swung round, pulling him over, he had instinctively slipped his other arm free and let go. He hadn't expected it to roll on such a slope but by the time he had regained his balance the rucksack was accelerating towards the boulder, which flipped it into the air and over the edge. While I had been preparing to mourn the death of my friend, he was coming to terms with the loss of his luggage.

Bivi-bag, sleeping bag, second camera, rope, wads of cash, grappling-hook, climbing gear, torch, two cassettes, both spoons; we ticked off the worst losses. They were serious but by no means life-threatening. We both knew we could get down somehow without the rope. The greatest disappointment lay with the two cassettes: irreplaceable footage of the mountain. Bruce also mourned the loss of his titanium grappling-hook. Apart from the cassettes, I regretted the absence of his bivi-bag most.

'I'm really sorry, mate. It'll only be for one night.'

Of course I didn't mind having to share a bag with him once more. I was far too pleased at not having to descend the rest of the mountain alone, with the image of my friend lying in the trees at the foot of that cliff running through my head.

In the cave we fashioned a set of spoons from a sliver of rock, and a tent peg wrapped in zinc-oxide tape. I still had my mug and cooker, but we had only half-a-block of hexamine left with which to heat up two meals. As he watched me eke out maximum cooking-power from the spluttering flame Bruce was contrite. Broken shoulder strap or no, his pride, as mine would have been, was sorely dented. I empathised but did, however, raise the subject of filming everything.

'I know, I know. I've been thinking of little else.' He laughed. 'Of course I don't want it to go on record - I'll get a right slating when we get home. I was just trying to decide what I'd be thinking if it had been your rucksack to go over.'

'You'd want to film it but you'd leave the final decision to me.'

'Yes I would.' He nodded gravely.

'And you'd do your utmost to persuade me.' My turn to laugh. 'And luckily there's a bit of juice left in one of the batteries.'

'Alright, alright. We'll go back to where it happened in the morning.'

We connected our jackets together for the tried and tested double-duvet but stopped short of stripping off again. Steam drifted out of the bag from our soaking trousers. Bruce was using his boots as a pillow, which meant they were less than four inches from my nose. There had to be some house rules. 'Here, use this instead.' I pushed over my bag of slings and karabiners and helped him kick the boots to the bottom of the bag.

'Mmm, luxury! What have you got?'

'My spare trousers.'

'What's that prodding my back?'

'My arm. It still stinks around here. What is it?'

'My socks. I've got them drying around me.'

'This is grim. How about a painkiller?'

'Top idea! Dish 'em out, then. All I've got left is some anti-histamine.'

'Don't they make you drowsy?'

We raced to dig out the bottles from our pockets. I dropped mine and heard the patter of pills hitting the ground sheet between us. Panic set in. 'Don't move!' It came out as a breathless squeak.

'Were those the codeine? Quick, they'll get wet!' Bruce tried to turn over, and the bivi-bag thrashed around in the mouth of the cave.

'Keep still! Where's the torch?'

'Here.' Bruce thrust it into my eye. 'Sorry!'

We dissolved into helpless laughter. I never did find those pills. By morning Bruce's socks had absorbed them. There were some left in the bottle anyway. The last thing I remember before a chemically-induced torpor numbed my brain was Bruce mumbling about not being able to film in the morning because the weather was always clear then and it had been cloudy when he lost his pack. If the Chihuahua thing living at the back of the cave came back I didn't hear it.

When I woke up there was light in the bag. I unzipped the door a bit further for a look and zipped it up again. The weather was perfect, misty and grey with drenching drizzle, the light exactly as it had been the previous afternoon.

So much rain had fallen overnight, running down the face of the cliffs above, that the basha sheet, spread out over a deep sink-hole at the mouth of the cave, had slipped out of sight under the weight of about five gallons of water. We retrieved it, then climbed back up to the spot where the rucksack had disappeared.

There was only enough battery power left to do one 'take' each so we had to get it right first time. I wasn't too happy about this. After all, I had to play the part of a man traumatised by the death and resurrection of his friend, all just a few minutes before. Bruce had only to play a man who had lost his luggage. Perhaps I should have done a dry run but it was too cold for rehearsals. As the recording light went out I felt I had overacted the emotions of the moment. During the actual event, apart from a few expletives, I had remained quite calm, unlike the gibbering, jelly-kneed wreck now stored for posterity on the cassette.

'Too late, battery's dead,' said Bruce.

Before leaving we cut the red basha sheet in two and hung one half over the edge of the cliff where the rucksack had disappeared. Neither of us enjoyed littering the mountainside in such a deliberate manner but, with luck, it would be a visible guide for any future search of the valley below, not that either of us had any intention of carrying it out. We wanted to be off this mountain and away from these valleys: sunlit oblivion at that Balinese pool-bar was calling.

'I'll post a reward and arrange collection through MAF,' Bruce concluded. (He did set this up but once out of the country he couldn't get a response from the relevant contacts and remains none the wiser as to whether any of his kit was ever found.)

We discussed at length the relative merits of different chocolate bars and cocktails as we made our way down the mountain towards base camp. At the upper of the two sections on which we had previously used a rope a new route had to be found. We split up to search, and I found one that was passable but tricky. Once more it was a small face of thick moss, peat and grass, with solid rock somewhere beneath. I had been stuck at the half-way point for a few minutes, stripping the rock of moss in the search for holds, when Bruce joined me having found no alternative. Rather than follow my own route he began to descend alongside it, just ten feet away.

From where I was, lower down, I could see it was not going

to work.

'Bruce, you're going to run out of holds there. Use this one - I'm almost there.'

'This'll be fine.'

It was not. He carried on, destroying each hold as he went until he was irrevocably stuck, unable to climb back up and with nowhere to go downwards. It was obvious to us both that he was going to fall – not far, five metres perhaps, and the ledge beneath was mossy enough to cushion the impact, but if he did not stop himself on that ledge the next drop would be longer and on to rocks, almost certainly a bone-breaker.

'At least wait until I'm down to catch you,' I spluttered.

But he lost his grip and fell, hit the ledge and rolled across it. My heart missed a beat as he reached the edge, hands flailing. Just as he seemed to be on the point of no return, he found a hold and stopped. He lay still for a second on his back, one arm hung out over the edge, looking up at me. Had he been wearing a rucksack he would have gone over.

'Parry, you're such a prat sometimes!'

'Come on, Anstice, get a move on! We'll miss last orders!'

We strode through the Hell's Arboretum as fast as the inefficiently cut path would allow. For old-time's sake I took passing swipes at any branch that looked as if it might irritate me. In the usual heavy rain and thick cloud the ground dropped away again, lone bushes drifting up towards us as we squelched through the spongy ground towards the top of the wall above camp one. Once again I lost all trace of our previous route.

'Sod this! Let's get the boys to come up and carry us down. I bet some of them are waiting at camp one.' Bruce pulled out his whistle and started blasting away into the mist. There was no answer but it was a good idea, worth pursuing, and we kept it up, whistling and shouting while we groped our way between the ghostly bushes. There was a good chance that at least some of the porters would have come up to camp one at this time of day in case we emerged. After seven days at base camp they must have been longing to get down off the mountain and keen to do anything that might speed our progress.

As the gradient steepened into the final section it was clear that we were in the wrong place. I lowered myself down on to a ledge and almost stepped into a void before discovering I could not get back up again. A shout from far below and to the right distracted Bruce from my predicament and he disappeared. For a while shouts and whistle blasts ricocheted back and forth through the murk.

'Simsun!' Whistle blast.

'Bruce!'

'Mr Mark, Mr Bruce!' More whistle blasts.

'Simsun!'

'Bruce, I'm stuck, dammit! Come and pull me out!'

'Simsun!'

I felt irrationally impatient. I too wanted to see Simsun. 'Bruce!' I yelled again. Goddammit, where was he?

'Yes! Where are you?' Bruce's voice drifted over from the right.

I had to wait while he extracted himself from a clump of bushes but eventually he was above me, hauling my pack up and helping me clamber after it. Simsun and Dalok were waiting below, at the top of the main face. They were just as pleased to see me as I was them. They looked freezing. They had left their T-shirts behind to keep them dry, and stood before us in shorts. Their bare feet squelched in the freezing moss as they stamped up and down, droplets of water pouring down their goose-pimpled skin and flying from their elbows as they shook my hand vigorously.

'Hand your pack over and let's get moving,' Bruce said. 'These boys are going to die in a minute.'

Simsun was already indicating he would take it and I put up no argument. Far be it from me to render a waste of time his efforts to get all the way up here.

They had found a different route up the face. It wasn't any less steep than ours but the various holds were in better condition and we followed them at a reckless pace. Without my rucksack I felt agile and invincible.

Camp one was as we had left it. It took just a few minutes to untie the lashings holding down the solar panels and the waterproof bag, then we were off again.

To keep warm Simsun and Dalok were moving at a hell of a rate, leaping fluidly from rock to tuft to root. To keep up I had to concentrate so hard on where my feet were landing that I lost all sense of time as we all but ran along the top of the spur. I only looked up when, after a few hours, I heard muffled voices. Simsun had stopped beside an odd-looking mound sitting just inside the tree-line and smoking gently into the mist, like a charcoal-burner's kiln. It took me a second to realise it was a new *pondok*. There was still some way to go before we would reach the base camp we had left a week before, and they had built themselves another, as high up the mountain as they could, sheathing it in bark in the absence of any decent-sized leaves. The low roof and overhanging eaves almost hid the piles of moss and branches that made up the walls. From the outside it looked wonderfully snug. And not a single man had left the party. Seven now filed out through the tiny door, grinning hugely.

'I'll pay these guys with my own money if need be,' Bruce said, of the four extra men, as we followed them back inside. 'I know we don't need them but I'm really touched that they stayed up here for so long.'

I was in full agreement. In another time and another place the obvious conclusion might have been that these men had hung around because they thought there would be something in it for them. I felt sure that was not the case. It appeared they had all been instructed to make sure we came to no harm. We had said at the start there would be no extra money. Well, there would be after all: the sum involved (£120 or thereabouts) was worth a few tankfuls of petrol back home but out here, to show our gratitude and appreciation, it was worth everything.

Inside the new base camp, they stoked up the fire and quizzed Simsun on how he had found us. Hot taro were pulled from the embers and thrust into our hands, our boots and socks were hung up in the smoke and one of the last pouches of tobacco was passed round. I noticed that in our absence not even a bag of this popular commodity had gone missing. Hunched shoulder to shoulder with them, blinking through the smoke, steam rising from drying clothes, we told them about the snow and the views at the top, the loss of Bruce's rucksack and the climbs. And what had they been up to, we asked. Oh, nothing much – a spot of hunting, building this hut. They laughed.

When darkness threatened we got around to setting up the basha sheet for water collection, and my bivi-bag.

'For once I'm envious of your sleeping arrangements,' Bruce said, as he helped me to tie up the sheet. 'How the hell are we all going to sleep in there?' He indicated the hut. 'There's only just enough room for everyone to sit!'

'You've got it in one,' I replied.

As I wrapped myself in my blanket and arranged a candle by the door of my snug cocoon to write by I could hear Bruce giggling at the crush of bodies trying to find sleeping positions in the hut. 'Please can I join you in there?' he called.

'Bugger off!'

3 March

Today we made it all the way to the two huts where the old man and boy left us. It was downhill, the only difficulty presenting itself when we stepped off our spur and made to cross the river crashing down from Long Drop Valley. It was no longer a little river: it was just what we had brought the grappling-hooks to deal with.

'We still haven't got any decent footage of the grappling-hooks being used and this would have been perfect,' Bruce wailed, above the roar of the water hurtling out of its gorge and into the Eilanden river on our right. I put up my hood against a renewed deluge of rain and pondered the options. It didn't look like an impossible crossing.

Simsun was standing near me and I motioned that perhaps we should climb back up into the trees and look for a crossing further upstream. He shook his head and pointed behind me. Several men were wrestling with the undergrowth already. I couldn't see them all but the swaying of branches and muffled shouts told a familiar story.

It was a bridge, of course. They lowered a pole across the first half of the torrent, jamming its end between two boulders, then two shimmied across, leapt into the second half and clawed their way powerfully to the other side. Within minutes the whole river was bridged, there was a handrail of sorts, and the men had formed a chain, standing in the water on the upstream side, bracing themselves against the wood and beckoning us on.

Only four of our companions are staying with the two of us in the larger of the two structures built at our last passing. Despite our protests, the rest are squeezed into the tiny lean-to shelter wedged under the overhanging boulder to give us more room to stretch out. Until everyone went to sleep we had only Simsun and Albias with us. We debated giving them a mug of chicken and pasta to share. To men unacquainted with any flavour stronger than burnt meat it was either going to be revolting or so mind-blowingly delicious that it would destroy their enjoyment of the local grub for ever.

'Their taro is going to go from top billing to slops status,' I remarked, stirring water into the saffron-coloured powder. 'Every meal after this will be misery for them. We can't do it to them.'

'But at least we won't feel so mean. I'm not sure I can handle eating this stuff in front of them any more, not after all they've done for us. With any luck they'll hate it.'

They loved it, I could tell, savouring every mouthful. The polished-clean mug was a dead give away too.

Then Simsun said it: '*Keladi* (taro) will never taste the same again.'

Thank God he had a smile on his face because we couldn't help laughing.

4 March

Bruce's mysterious illness is back, with a vengeance this time. He was so much his old self on the mountain that I had forgotten about it. Was it a fluke that he felt okay when it really mattered, or was it altitude and its effect on the blood that beat back whatever it is? We both think the former would be too much of a coincidence and that he has a blood disease. It can't be malaria – he has none of the usual symptoms. We'll know soon enough. We're just a day's walk from the airstrip. This adventure is almost at an end and I'm not sure how I feel about it. Part of me wants to get out of here. I crave good food, and Bruce isn't much fun when he's ill, but ever since we booked the Cessna I have been building up to a date rather than an event. That date is now only three days away. I expect to go home: I can visualise home and all its comforts as tantalisingly close. But the problems with the police that may well lie ahead mean that 'tantalising' rather than 'close' is probably the operative word.

The rest of me is sad that we're not heading into the white patches on the map.

19 BACK TO THE TWENTY-FIRST CENTURY

5 March

The welcome we received in Tabasik was ecstatic. One old woman, lurching out of her hut, even threw her arms round each of us in turn. Everyone had been fearful for our safety on *Abom*. The women clucked around us as we dropped our loads by the men's hut, pinching my scrawny arms and expressing shock at how thin we were. We had been skin and bone on display at the party a fortnight ago but were death's door material now.

Amid the hubbub Bruce discovered that the *kepala desa* had flown from Sumtamun to Wamena for a 'meeting' and wasn't expected back for two days. I digested this information with alarm. 'He'll almost certainly have kicked up a fuss there over our having paid someone else for permission to climb his mountain,' Bruce said, as if I needed it spelt out. 'I think we now have to assume that the authorities know we are here.'

'He'll be flying back on the same plane that's picking us up.'

'Yes, but I don't think the authorities would come all the way out here. They're more likely to be waiting for us in Wamena. If he's told them we've got a TV camera we're buggered.'

'He won't have. Why should he? There's nothing he could gain from it,' I said hopefully.

My thoughts were interrupted by the *Bapa Tua* who had lamented the passing of *Abom's* icecap. Clutching my arm he led me to the edge of the spur and I thought he was going to convey something momentous to me, a pearl of wisdom. He pointed up at the bunches of green bananas hanging from a palm and fixed my eyes with his. I held my breath.

'*Uang!*' he croaked.

'What? *Uang*? Oh, money! You want me to buy your bananas?'

We were both disappointed. They were probably very good bananas and I was in dire need of nourishment but they were the indigestible type we loathed and he couldn't have been more misguided.

I will never forget the send-off we received from the people of Tabasik. They lined the path out of the village and down towards the trees, and, to the last child, they shook and clung to our hands. It was a display of hospitality and warmth from relative strangers that I had only rarely experienced before, pure friendship and goodwill. One or two of the girls, I thought, looked particularly sad to see us go but that was probably just my ego: compared to the healthy, athletic young local men we were pathetic specimens.

The topic of conversation en route to Sumtamun rarely left the problems that might be in store for us at Wamena. Even if nobody was waiting for us as we climbed out of the Cessna we would have to show our *surat jalans*, travel permits, there, if only to arrange the flight onwards to Jayapura, the capital of Irian Jaya. What would happen when the police saw how out-of-date they were and that there was no entry stamp for the area?

'They won't see mine at all,' Bruce remarked airily. 'It's in my rucksack. Perhaps you should 'lose' yours too.'

'I think it would be better at least to show we had them to start with. I could smudge it so it's recognisable but not legible.'

'Yes - soak it. We got lost and had a terrible time with a river. That's how I lost my pack. We were trying to get from Senggo to Wamena and went up the wrong river. We've been weeks, no, months in the jungle. Christ, look at the state of us. They can't not believe us.' I hadn't yet seen myself in a mirror but Bruce had a point: bearded, gaunt and filthy, he did look sort of distressed.

'That's fine if they don't know we've just arrived from Sumtamun,' I countered. 'But if they do know that, then either they were waiting for us anyway, thanks to the *kepala desa*, or we'll have had to go through some kind of control point after we get out of the Cessna. In which case whatever's wrong with our *surat jalans* is academic. They'll know we've been in a restricted area. And as to that, we don't even know if it *is* a restricted area. It might be perfectly OK to fly in from Sumtamun.'

'The only thing we *do* know is that we haven't got one inch of footage that's likely to upset the authorities. But that's not going to help us either. They're not going to trawl through fifty hours of footage to find out. Once they've confiscated the tapes we'll never get them back.'

'The real problem will be when we're searched. Do you think they'll search us?'

'Definitely.'

'Me too. How about we pay for someone else to come on the flight and get the black box and the sat-phone through? We can take out a few innocuous tapes and keep them with the camera. He can carry the box and phone inside something else and pretend to have nothing to do with us. We could even safeguard the camera by carrying lots of blank tapes and saying that the humidity broke it early on. They'd be less likely to nick it then. We could even put water in it - dry it out later.' As I rattled this off I thought it was the start of an excellent plan. Permits or no permits, I didn't believe that too much trouble was going to come our way if we could get away with being lost tourists. Perhaps we might be pushed around and questioned for a while, made to pay a 'fine' or have the camera confiscated, but I was fairly confident that would be all. We must have the camera on us in case they already knew of its existence. There wouldn't be time at the other end of this flight to reassess and then start swapping things around. It was only the black box and the satellite phone that would almost certainly land us in serious trouble. The phone was enough on its own: we hadn't declared it. The addition of an extra box and the sheer number of tapes inside it turned the camera from a tourist toy into a media weapon. The chance of the officer discovering them on two people flying in from the east, without permits or visas, and not thinking we were something to do with the OPM guerrillas was virtually nil.

'Simsun?' Bruce looked at me askance.

'Probably. It would have to be someone who knew exactly

what they were doing and he's the only one who...' I tailed off realising suddenly what I was suggesting.

'We'd be asking him to become a smuggler.'

Of course we couldn't. Ours was hardly a noble cause. I felt guilty for having thought of putting Simsun at risk. Even though he might have done it for a good price we would never know if he understood the risks, or even what to do if Bruce and I were waylaid on landing. Also, the Cessna was probably only going to be a four-seater, in which case the pilot would undoubtedly grasp that our accomplice was no stranger to us.

'Okay, then. What about we leave the box and phone here and get someone else to come back and collect them when we know the coast is clear? We might even find we can do it ourselves.'

'That's what I was thinking. We'd need to get our hands on more money, of course, but the question is where do we leave it? The only people we know and trust are from Tabasik, and they live too far away for whoever we send to grab the kit and return on the same plane.'

There was going to be no easy solution, but at least we had a whole day in Sumtamun to come up with a plan before the MAF Cessna roared up the valley. Before we settled into the hut we had used before, we paid a visit to the radio operator to confirm this.

'*Cessna   tidak*   No!   *Helicopter   datang! Wokawokawokawokawoka...*'

Once more, his crazed laughter followed us out of the door.

6 March

As the last of the morning's steam rising from the grassy slopes around Sumtamun was sucked skywards, I wandered down to the river running alongside the airstrip to wash my clothes. The sun was barely above the hills and already it was soporifically hot. It wouldn't do to arrive in Wamena looking and smelling like a caveman. No matter where you are in Asia, or the world for that matter, if there's petty bureaucracy to be dealt with, it pays dividends to look your best. In this case my best wasn't going to be up to much. My green shirt still looked fairly respectable but both sets of trousers were torn, and covered all over with blood-red blotches of betadine solution that wouldn't come out. Great rolls of dirt came off my skin.

I was ponderously laying out everything to dry on the grass outside our hut when the unmistakable drone of an engine buzzed through the air. Its unfamiliarity stood out so starkly above the classroom chatter emanating from the school that I was looking down the valley for its source long before the little white speck appeared low above the trees, climbing up the valley floor towards the airstrip. 'Shit!' I snatched up my washing and yelled, 'Bruce, the plane's here.'

Inside the hut, every bag was unpacked. We had been sorting out what we had left to trade. Bruce started throwing things we no longer needed out of the door. Several men ran to inform us that the plane had arrived. I brandished the cooking-pot over everything that was now lying in the dirt. In the heat of the moment the correct Indonesian escaped me.

'*Bagus* – good - stuff! *Uang tidak! Saya mau kampok* Batu, *nocken*...No money, I want stone axes, bags...' I mimed bows and arrows and they ran off. The plane was going to have to wait for a while.

Within fifteen minutes our bags were packed and we were bundling up the new booty with string, watched by a crowd of onlookers. There were still people arriving with stuff to trade, but the dealing was over. Without being asked, Simsun and Albias grabbed everything but two bags and headed down to the airstrip. I disengaged myself from a man who wanted to exchange a ragged bundle of arrows for my *parang* - one article I wasn't letting go of – and we followed. A man dressed incongruously in a shiny white shell-suit with purple trim was walking up the hill towards us flanked by two others. It was the *kepala desa* of Tabasik. My heart skipped a beat as I suddenly remembered our potential predicament, but the two men with him were not policemen. I watched his face as Bruce told him of our success, how great Simsun and the boys had been, and how grateful we were to the people of Tabasik and Biblangda. Farewells were said and we continued towards the plane.

'Well, that wasn't very encouraging.' Bruce said.

'I know. Did you notice that he could barely look either of us in the eye?'

Bruce agreed. 'How stupid are we going to feel walking into such an obvious trap? Where's the phone?'

'Right down at the bottom of my pack.'

The black box was disguised as a bundle of grass skirts and string bags inside one of the polypropylene sacks. The orange box was unhidden and intrigue-free.

'I think we'll get a feel for what's afoot before we've unpacked the plane. Maybe we can hide something on board as if we left it by mistake and go back for it later. Or maybe you can grab the controls and fly us across the border.' He laughed. 'Make a great finale to the film.'

Our pilot was a tall American called Peter. He counted out our payment and manoeuvred the huge bundle of bows and arrows into the hold of the Cessna as we said goodbye to Simsun and Albias.

'Looks like you two have had a helluva journey,' Peter said, as he climbed into the front seat beside me. 'It'll be gettin' quite bumpy bout now. I'm sure you boys aren't the gettin'-sick kind but I have to ask you not to eat anything during the flight because you're liable to bring it right back up.'

We had barely climbed out of the valley when I turned to talk to Bruce in the back seat and found him sniggering into a mug of noodles. He put a finger to his lips and pushed the camera at me.

I asked Peter if he would fly us over Mandala before he turned westwards towards Wamena but he didn't have enough fuel. As I watched the cloud swell over its south-eastern flanks I realised that in any case we were unlikely to get a good view of our route. It was hard to equate the rolling cloth of green below us with the reality of the journey Bruce and I had just undertaken. As we banked right in a wide turn round the southern foothills I could already see the bend in the Eilanden river, near which we had made our exhausting crossing to Kowet. The silvery slash through the otherwise unrelenting green looked peaceful and harmless. Further to the south-west the unbroken canopy of the Korowai region gave no indication of the complex human society existing there as it had done for perhaps thousands of years. Somewhere down there was the family whose afternoon we had so rudely interrupted less than two months before. Already it felt a lifetime ago. The twenty-first century roar of the engine shunted that experience into the realms of fiction. At the time, with my rucksack, clothes and boots on, I had felt like an alien invader. Now I was back in my spaceship, where I belonged, looking but not seeing, and not interfering.

The tectonic chaos was all but invisible from up here. I couldn't see the mud, or the dank, spray-slicked, treacherous gorges, or where broadleaf gave way to moss forest. Where the alpine scrub and rocky crags of the higher peaks might have appeared, there was only cloud. The only clue to the reality of passing on foot among those hills was the abruptness of every slope and the sharpness of every angle. It seemed impossible that trees could cling to such gradients. The Cessna lurched sickeningly in a thermal then plunged and I swung the camera around, hoping to catch a noodle disaster in Bruce's lap. No such luck – he laughed into the lens.

The hillside Dani settlements on the approach into the Baliem valley were markedly different from the Una ones we had left behind. Tidy clusters of two or three beehive huts sat penned inside neat brushwood fences. The slopes were less dramatic and the terraced fields looked more organised and lush. Life here appeared less harsh. No wonder the Dani had had so much time to develop the flamboyant rituals and mock warfare that had put them on the tourist map as soon as the anthropologists and missionaries had done their bit. And then the unkempt concrete sprawl of Wamena was in front of us.

The plane taxied into a small parking lot at the MAF headquarters. I scanned the buildings for police but none appeared. Bruce jumped out and walked through the building to see if there was a checkpoint on the other side. He returned visibly relieved. 'There's nothing between here and the street. I'll go and check the main terminal.'

I stayed in the MAF compound, scrounging sacks and string to make our bundles of bows and arrows more aircraft-friendly. I felt more confident now. Perhaps, after all, we were going to get through this unscathed.

But an hour passed and there was still no sign of him. Had someone asked to see his passport and *surat jalan*? Was he now sitting in a police station? I couldn't risk ferrying everything to the terminal and inviting closer scrutiny of our bags until I knew. Eventually I found someone to look after it all and walked warily up the road to find out.

Bruce was skulking just inside the departures and arrivals hall. He looked jumpy. 'There you are!' he said. 'I thought you'd run into trouble. I've been questioned twice on where we've come from - there are police everywhere. Where's the kit? I've got us a flight in two hours' time. Here, look, have some of this.' He held out a paper bag full of chocolate and buns.

'It might have escaped your notice but there's too much for one person to carry. I thought you were the one in trouble.'

We left the kit where it was and I went out to buy more chocolate.

At first glance we were in a normal Indonesian provincial town; single and double-storey concrete shops and offices, with steel reinforcing-rods protruding messily from the rooftops, waiting for extra levels to be added; taxis, buses and cycle rickshaws jostling with pedestrians along the ragged Tarmac of the road. The people told a different story, however. Those behind the green-, beige- and blue-washed shop fronts were all Indonesians, while those milling around on the streets with no obvious signs of employment, and the rickshaw drivers, were Irianese. This was a colonial town, the line between the haves and the have-nots following closely the race division between colonialists and colonised.

I had not thought of anyone we met as being poor since we had left the Asmat. Materially they might have been, but they had all seemed content and healthy, their traditional existence, new-found religion, and dependence on themselves and the land providing all they wished for and could expect from life. There was poverty here, though. I knew it was not indicative of the Baliem valley in general but everywhere I looked there were Dani men and women in their traditional garb of penis gourds and grass or bead skirts, looking at odds with their surroundings. On a street corner an elderly man, a once proud warrior, sifted through a pile of rubbish. A woman with a child sat on a step, begging. Others made their way towards me clutching bundles of woven cane bracelets and freshly made bone daggers with pleading looks on their faces. At times theirs might be a lucrative business but I had seen only one other tourist in the last hour.

At last we could delay ferrying our equipment into the terminal building no longer. Our flight was about to depart. Almost immediately a policeman marched up to us, kicked the polypropylene sack containing the black box and demanded to see what was inside. My heart sank. We were so close: I could see our aeroplane through the windows. There were no X-ray machines between it and us, and once we were on it we would be safe. Bruce stalled him with excited babble about bows and arrows while I opened the sack and showed him the mound of string bags within.

'*Surat jalan?* Travel permit?' he barked.

I pretended not to understand. It was better that Bruce came up with a story – whichever one he felt was most appropriate. As Bruce answered I tried to distract our tormentor, pulling out one of the string bags and thrusting it enthusiastically into his face as if he might want to appreciate its quality. He waved it away. Then I realised that Bruce wasn't spinning a tale of rivers sweeping away bits of paper: he was asking the man if he knew of any recent football scores. It was a stroke of genius: Indonesia is fanatical about football.

'Which team?' asked the policeman.

'Manchester United.'

'Aah.' The man's face broke into a delighted grin. 'Ryan Giggs!'

'Yeah, yeah! Ryan Giggs!' we chorused. *'Bagus sekali!* Very good!'

We swapped footballers' names for a while, throwing in any we knew. I had no idea which teams they all played for but it didn't matter. Our new friend walked away still muttering reverently, 'Ryan Giggs.'

As far as our concerns over the authorities lay we appeared to be all but home and dry. Once in Jayapura, waiting for an onward flight to Bali, there was little likelihood of our papers being checked. Nobody there, or anywhere else until we flew out of Jakarta, need have any suspicion that we had been anywhere we shouldn't. The three businessmen who took their places with us in the small jet-liner, in which all but ten seats in the tail had been ripped out to carry fuel drums, looked disparagingly at our stained clothing and unruly facial hair. The baggage we had been so concerned about was flung through the same door and lashed to the oily remnants of the gangway carpeting by a man who grinned at us and mimed firing an arrow. As the wheels left the Tarmac we toasted our success with a can of warm Sprite, congratulating each other on what felt like a narrow escape.

The low-altitude flight north crossed our originally intended route from Mandala to the coast and took just under an hour. Staring out of the window, I tried to get a feel for what our journey might have been like, scanning the flat expanse of forest, stretching from horizon to horizon, for any signs of human habitation. Occasionally a small clearing appeared but I never saw any roofs. The red-brown scar of a vehicle-track hinted at the presence of the lumber industry, but otherwise there was nothing visible from that height but trees. I ought to have been able to see the Idenburg, the big river we had planned to use as an escape route if things got ugly, but I must have turned my head at the wrong moment.

For the first time since Bruce had asked me to accompany him on this expedition I was without a sense of impending adventure. It was an odd feeling but one tempered by a new excitement – we had some outstanding film footage and I was itching to begin writing my first book. This expedition had lived up to every promise and looked set to influence my life for years to come.

'What a fantastic trip,' said Bruce. 'Definitely the best thing I've ever done. Where do you think our next one should be?'

'I don't know. The list is long. We've still got to cross that one day.' I indicated the forest below as the plane bounced through a patch of turbulence.

'Sooner than you think, mate. Look.'

Through the cockpit door both pilots had their hands in the air and were screaming.

'*Bodoh* – idiots,' said the man next to Bruce.

EPILOGUE

On arrival in Jayapura, Irian Jaya's capital, we saw ourselves in a mirror for the first time in seventy-seven days. It was a shock. There were no scales but I could not have weighed much more than eight stones – I had started the trip at just under eleven. Later, while Bruce was being sick for the third time that day, I ate his supper. On arrival in Bali the following day he had time for one dip in the hotel swimming pool before being convulsed with violent shivers. The hospital diagnosed vivax malaria, and the more dangerous cerebral strain, falciparum. I picked him up a week later when his fever had been brought under control and an hour later was shivering over a cocktail in the scorching sun; I had vivax too. Before flying to Jakarta and on to London we managed one celebratory meal together. There were two toasts, to the best trip of our lives, and to holding the food down. In the following months, an exhausted Bruce suffered attack after attack. Excited specialists in London and Hamburg suggested that malaria had been the cause of his illness all along, and that his accustomed immune system – he had had it before – had hidden the usual symptoms. He also had salmonella and worms. If Bruce Parry says he is ill, he is ill.

One year later Bruce was crossing Ethiopia's Danakil desert in the footsteps of Sir Wilfred Thesiger. The only remaining sign of Maverick Travel was debt and I was back in the jungle, this time in Central America. I had already helped a friend set a new mountaineering record in Europe and was about to take up roped-access work in London to make ends meet between trips. Abseiling down a building is no substitute for climbing a mountain but the confines of my eight-foot-by-five-foot office remain a distant memory. Bruce and I have not yet been on another trip together, but there's plenty of time.

GLOSSARY

abom - Una name for Gunung Mandala
anak-anak - children
awas - careful
bagus - good
bahasa - language
bahaya - dangerous
bakar - roast, bake
banyak - much, many
bapa tua - old man, old Sir
bapak, bapa - dad, father, Mr, Sir
basar - big
basha sheet - awning used as rain shelter (origin British military)
bechara - talk
belum - not yet
bisa - able, can
bisj - ancestor pole
bivi bag - Gore-Tex bivouac bag
bodoh - idiot
bua mera - a red fruit prized for its dye, and as a vegetable
bulay - Westerner
camat - local government-appointed village official
cassowary - large flightless bird, the largest animal indigenous to
    Irian Jaya
cessna - light aircraft
datang - arrive
di atas - above
di mana - where
di sana - (over) there
dingin - cold
dulu - first

dynamic rope - climbing rope with stretch designed to absorb shock-loading

enak - delicious

engkau - you

es - ice

gaharu - scented wood used in the production of incense (Aquilaria mallaccensis)

GPS - Global Positioning System satellite navigation handset

gunung - mountain

hutan - forest

Inggris - English

jalan - path,street

jamasj - war shield (Asmat)

jau - far

jeu - longhouse (Asmat)

juta - million

kakhua - witch, sorcerer (Korowai)

kampok batu - stone axe

kecil - small

keladi - taro (Una)

kepala desa - village chief

kohat - strong

laleo - evil spirit (Korowai)

ma'af - sorry

MAF - Missionary Aviation Fellowship (Protestant)

makan - to eat

masalah - problem

masuk - enter

matti - dead

mau - want

mereka - they

merpati - pigeon

nama - name

nocken - string bag (Una)

orang - people

pagi - morning

parang - jungle knife, machete

PELNI - Pelayaran Nasional Indonesia (the national passenger shipping line)
peta - map
polis - police
pondok - hut
pulang - go home
puncak - peak (mountain)
rattan - a plant family, some species of which are used as rope or string
rumah laki-laki - men's hut
sago - the staple food of the lowland Irianese
sali - grass skirt (Una)
saya - I, me, mine
sekali - very
selamat pagi - good morning
semua - every
senang - happy
static rope - pre-stretched rope
stenga - half
sungai - river
surat jalan - travel permit
terima kasih - thank you
tidak - no
tingal - stay, leave as is
tuan - Sir
uang - money
udang - shrimp
win - pandanus nuts (Una)
ya - yes

About Eye Books

Eye books is a young, dynamic publishing company that likes to break the rules. Our independence allows us to publish books which challenge the way people see things. It also means that we can offer new authors a platform from which they can shine their light and encourage others to do the same.

To date we have published 30 books that cover a number of genres including Travel, Biography, Adventure and History. Many of our books are experience driven. All of them are inspirational and life-affirming.

Frigid Women, for example, tells the story of the world-record making first all female expedition to the North Pole. A fifty year-old mother of three who had recently recovered from a mastectomy, and her daughter are the authors neither had ever written a book before. Sue Riches is now both author and highly sought after motivational speaker.

We also publish thematic anthologies, such as The Tales from Heaven and Hell series, for those who prefer the short story format. Here everyone has the chance to get their stories published and win prizes such as flights to any destination in the world.

And here's what makes us really different: As well as publishing books, Eye Books has set up a club for like-minded people and is in the process of developing a number of initiatives and services for its community of members. After all, the more you put into life, the more you get out of it.

Please visit www.eye-books.com for further information.

Eye Club Membership

Each month, we receive hundreds of enquiries' from people who have read our books, discovered our website or entered our competitions. All of these people have certain things in common; a desire to achieve, to extend the boundaries of everyday life and to learn from others' experiences.

Eye Books has, therefore, set up a club to unite these like-minded people. It is a community where members can exchange ideas, contact authors, discuss travel, both future and past as well as receive information and offers from ourselves.

Membership is free.

Benefits of the Eye Club

As a member of the Eye Club:

• You are offered the invaluable opportunity to contact our authors directly.
• You will be able to receive a regular newsletter, information on new book releases and company developments as well as discounts on new and past titles.
• You can attend special member events such as book launches, author talks and signings.
• Receive discounts on a variety of travel related products and services from Eye Books partners.
• In addition, you can enjoy entry into Eye Books competitions including the ever popular Heaven and Hell series and our monthly book competition.

To register your membership, simply visit our website and register on our club pages: www.eye-books.com.

New Titles

Riding the Outlaw Trail - Simon Casson

A true story of an epic horseback journey by two Englishmen from Mexico to Canada, across 2,000 miles of some of America's most difficult terrain. Their objective? To retrace the footsteps of those legendary real life bandits Butch Cassidy and the Sundance Kid, by riding the outlaw trails they rode more than a century ago.
ISBN: 1 903070 228. Price £9.99.

Desert Governess - Phyllis Ellis

Phyllis, a former Benny Hill actress, takes on a new challenge when she becomes a governess to the Saudi Arabian Royal family. In this frank personal memoir, she gives us an insider's view into the Royal family and a woman's role in this mysterious kingdom.
ISBN: 1 903070 015. Price £9.99.

Last of the Nomads - W. J. Peasley

Warri and Yatungka were the last of the desert nomads to live permanently in the traditional way. Their deaths marked the end of a tribal lifestyle that stretched back more than 30,000 years. The Last of the Nomads tells of an extraordinary journey in search of Warri and Yatungka, their rescue and how they survived alone for thirty years in the unrelenting Western Desert region of Australia.
ISBN: 1 903070 325. Price £9.99.

All Will Be Well - Michael Meegan

So many self help books look internally to provide inspiration, however this book looks at how love and compassion when given out to others, can act as a better antidote to the human condition than trying to inwardly solve feelings of discontentment.
ISBN: 1 903070 279. Price £9.99.

Travellers' Tales From Heaven and Hell Part 3 - Various
This is the third book in the series, after the first two best selling
Travellers' Tales from Heaven and Hell. It is an eclectic collection
of over a hundred anecdotal travel stories which will enchant you,
shock you and leave you in fits of laughter!
ISBN: 1 903070 112. Price £9.99.

Special Offa - Bob Bibby
Following his last best selling book Dancing with Sabrina, Bob
walks the length of Offa's Dyke. He takes us through the towns
and villages that have sprung up close by and reveals their
ancient secrets and folklore. He samples the modern day with his
refreshingly simple needs and throws light on where to go and
what to see.
ISBN: 1 903070 287. Price £9.99.

No Socks No Sex - Gail Haddock
Armed with a beginner's guide to surgery, GP Gail Haddock took
up her VSO posting at a remote hospital in Sierra Leone. As she set
off into the unknown, action, adventure and romance were high on
her agenda; rebel forces and the threat of civil war were not.
ISBN: 1 903070 295. Price £9.99.

The Good Life - Dorian Amos
Needing a change and some adventure, Dorian and his wife
searched their world atlas and decided to sell up and move to
Canada. Having bought Pricey the car, Boris Lock their faithful dog,
a canoe and their fishing equipment they set off into the Yukon
Wilderness to find a place they could call home.
ISBN: 1 903070 309. Price £9.99.

Baghdad Business School - Heyrick Bond Gunning

A camp bed, ten cans of baked beans, some water and $25,000 is all that was needed to set up an International Business in Iraq. The book chronicles an amusing description of the trials and tribulations of doing business in an environment where explosions and shootings are part of everyday life, giving the reader a unique insight into what is really happening in this country.

ISBN: 1 903070 333. Price £9.99.

The Con Artists Handbook - Joel Levy

Get wise with The Con Artist's Handbook as it blows the lid on the secrets of the successful con artist and his con games. Get inside the hustler's head and find out what makes him tick; Learn how the world's most infamous scams are set up and performed; Peruse the career profiles of the most notorious scammers and hustlers of all time; Learn to avoid the modern-day cons of the e-mail and Internet age.

ISBN: 1 903070 341. Price £9.99.

The Forensics Handbook - Pete Moore

The Forensic Handbook is the most up-to-date log of forensic techniques available. Discover how the crime scene is examined using examples of some of the most baffling crimes; Learn techniques of lifting, comparing and identifying prints; Calculate how to examine blood splatter patterns; Know what to look for when examining explosive deposits, especially when terrorist activity is suspected.

Learn how the Internet is used to trace stalkers.

ISBN: 1 903070 35X. Price £9.99.

Also by Eye Books

Jasmine and Arnica - Nicola Naylor
A blind woman's journey around India.
ISBN: 1 903070 171. Price £9.99.

Touching Tibet - Niema Ash
A journey into the heart of this intriguing forbidden kingdom.
ISBN: 1 903070 18X. Price £9.99.

Behind the Veil - Lydia Laube
A shocking account of a nurses Arabian nightmare.
ISBN: 1 903070 198. Price £9.99.

Walking Away - Charlotte Metcalf
A well known film makers African journal.
ISBN: 1 903070 201. Price £9.99.

Travels in Outback Australia - Andrew Stevenson
In search of the original Australians - the Aboriginal People.
ISBN: 1 903070 147. Price £9.99

The European Job - Jonathan Booth
10,000 miles around Europe in a 25 year old classic car.
ISBN: 1 903070 252. Price £9.99

Around the World with 1000 Birds - Russell Boyman
An extraordinary answer to a mid-life crisis.
ISBN: 1 903070 163. Price £9.99

Cry from the Highest Mountain - Tess Burrows
A climb to the point furthest from the centre of the earth.
ISBN: 1 903070 120. Price £9.99

Dancing with Sabrina - Bob Bibby
A journey from source to sea of the River Severn.
ISBN: 1 903070 244. Price £9.99

Grey Paes and Bacon - Bob Bibby
A journey around the canals of the Black Country
ISBN: 1 903070 066. Price £7.99

Jungle Janes - Peter Burden
Twelve middle-aged women take on the Jungle. As seen on Ch 4.
ISBN: 1 903070 05 8. Price £7.99

Travels with my Daughter - Niema Ash
Forget convention, follow your instincts.
ISBN: 1 903070 04 X. Price £7.99

Riding with Ghosts - Gwen Maka
One woman's solo cycle ride from Seattle to Mexico.
ISBN: 1 903070 00 7. Price £7.99

Riding with Ghosts: South of the Border - Gwen Maka
The second part of Gwen's epic cycle trip across the Americas.
ISBN: 1 903070 09 0. Price £7.99

Triumph Round the World - Robbie Marshall
He gave up his world for the freedom of the road.
ISBN: 1 903070 08 2. Price £7.99

Fever Trees of Borneo - Mark Eveleigh
A daring expedition through uncharted jungle.
ISBN: 0 953057 56 9. Price £7.99

Discovery Road - Tim Garrett and Andy Brown
Their mission was to mountain bike around the world.
ISBN: 0 953057 53 4. Price £7.99

Frigid Women - Sue and Victoria Riches
The first all-female expedition to the North Pole.
ISBN: 0 953057 52 6. Price £7.99

Jungle Beat - Roy Follows
Fighting Terrorists in Malaya.
ISBN: 0 953057 57 7. Price £7.99

Slow Winter - Alex Hickman
A personal quest against the backdrop of the war-torn Balkans.
ISBN: 0 953057 58 5. Price £7.99

Tea for Two - Polly Benge
She cycled around India to test her love.
ISBN: 0 953057 59 3. Price £7.99

Traveller's Tales from Heaven and Hell - Various
A collection of short stories from a nationwide competition.
ISBN: 0 953057 51 8. Price £6.99

More Traveller's Tales from Heaven and Hell - Various
The second collection of short stories.
ISBN: 1 903070 02 3. Price £6.99

A Trail of Visions: Route 1 - Vicki Couchman
A stunning photographic essay.
ISBN: 1 871349 338. Price £14.99

A Trail of Visions: Route 2 - Vicki Couchman
The second stunning photographic essay.
ISBN: 0 953057 50 X. Price £16.99

Book Microsites

If you are interested in finding out more about this book please visit our book microsite:

www.eye-books.com/firstcontact/home.htm

We have also created microsites for a number of our other new books including:

Riding The Outlaw Trail
Desert Governess
The Last of the Nomads
Special Offa
The Good Life
No Socks No Sex
Baghdad Business School

For details on these sites and others which we are developing please visit our main website:

www.eye-books.com

Special Offers and Promotions

We are offering our club members and people who have read this book the opportunity to take advantage of promotions on our other books by buying direct from us.

For information on these special offers please visit the following page of our website:

www.eye-books.com/promotions.htm